CW00538615

The Secret Christmas

☆

The Secret Christmas

Edited by

Terence Handley MacMath

DARTON · LONGMAN + TODD

First published in Great Britain in 1990 by
Darton, Longman and Todd Ltd
1 Spencer Court
140 – 142 Wandsworth High Street
London SW18 4JJ

This edition published 2013
Introduction and arrangement
© 2013 Terence Handley MacMath

ISBN 978–0–232–53023–0

A catalogue record for this book is available from the British Library

Phototypeset by Kerrypress Ltd, Luton, Bedfordshire.
Printed and bound by Bell & Bain Ltd, Glasgow.

Contents

To Eleanor Robinson and Trinity Handley MacMath
- the Christmas Fairies

Introduction

Most people keep two Christmases – one blazing with greens, reds and gold, a public-spirited, family affair, for which whole factories labour all year round to provide the paper Santa Clauses, crackers, displays and designs for every conceivable domestic item at Christmas time. It is the Christmas the new employers, the Puritans, banned as an uncommercial proposition – their gifts of prophecy failed them here – and an undignified, unholy row. It is the Christmas we love to hate, complete with a hundred horrid chores, unwanted relations and Bing Crosby crooning in every department store.

The other Christmas is secret – blue and silvery white for those who have the eyes for that kind of thing, but for most, a fleeting sense of joy and wonder which touches them when the horror of the office party is safely over, and when there is an oasis of quiet in the family celebrations: midnight mass; the King's College service of Nine Lessons and Carols on the radio; the first glimpse of the Christmas tree in all its glory. It provides the impulse for crusty business men to find small change for the caterwauling urchins carolling at their front doors, and keeps the weary housewives trudging through their preparations.

This is not to say that the first kind of Christmas is not immense fun, but only to say that the second is more precious, and it is what gives the first its joy. If the unimaginably great power behind the universe could love us so much as to become one of us, not in spirit only, but with all the limitations and narrowness that constrain us in our finite, human bodies – then we are loved indeed. To put it in Christian terms: if God could choose freely to become a human – who happened to be a man called Jesus, or Joshua, son of a carpenter, born in a stable, living in an occupied, backward country – then humans are infinitely valuable.

For those who cannot hold God within such a humanly recognizable form, then still, there is a sense that at Christmas, humanity becomes lovable. The claims of the poor, the cold, the homeless, the sad, demand relief. A charity like Crisis (formerly Crisis at Christmas) tugs at people's heartstrings because it is indeed a crisis if at Christmas, of all times, there is hunger and homelessness. Christmas is a celebration of our worth and preciousness – if not to God, then to each other.

Crisis properly means not 'emergency' – a problem to which we must make a response. The true meaning of the word is 'turning point' – a choice we must make. Christmas comes at the turning point of the year; it marks the turning point in God's relations with us. It is a yearly reminder of the choices we are continually forced to make between loving or refusing to love; accepting or refusing to accept. The work of Crisis is not over at Christmas, of course, and nor are our own opportunities to love the people around us. But Christmas – like the baby in the manger – makes ideas of love tangible, and translates them into presents of our time, skills and money.

This collection of prose and poetry for Christmas holds these two themes in mind: the secret, private response of people to Christmas, and the impulse to give which lies at the heart of Christmas, remembering as it does, the gift of God himself to us. There are a few sad and distressing pieces; the Christmas message brings joy to the world, but Christmas itself can heighten the wretchedness of some human circumstances. It promises goodwill from God to all people and between all men and women on earth; that promise is still to be brought to perfect fruition.

Since this collection was first put together, the world has darkened even more for most of us. The Boxing Day tsunami in 2004 took the tinsel out of millions of people's Christmas fantasies, even though they may have known no one directly affected by the disaster. That such a thing could happen when the world was waiting joyfully to hear again that message of the angels, 'goodwill from heaven to all people' seemed a particularly shattering betrayal of trust. Terrorism, economic recession, climate chaos and the loss of trust in each other, from politicians, priests and bankers to family entertainers eats away at our basic sense that all is well with the world. And then there are the personal losses: if I had a pound for every time I listened to someone saying, 'We're not really having Christmas this year … not now x has happened', I'd be able to fulfil my childhood fantasies of a Hamley's-style Christmas every day of the year. Crisis tells us that homelessness, particularly of children and young people, rises after families, already under pressure, break under unrealistic expectations about the Christmas break.

Of course, the actual Christmas event was a rough-and-ready affair, surrounded by fear and violence. Perhaps the joy of Christmas now is always to be found in those unexpected moments when we perceive the divine presence dropping in, as it were, for a vist – as Simon Parke did one Christmas in a bleak supermarket warehouse – and a light is born in our hearts which is at once instantly recognisable, utterly fresh and new. This can't be bought, or sought, and it happens as often in moments of sorrow as of joy. All we are asked is to keep an open door.

TERENCE HANDLEY MACMATH

☆

Advent

Advent Prayer

O Lord, again with the turning of the year we begin our pilgrimage toward Christmas. Our hearts as ever rejoice in the glad tidings of Christ who is born in Bethlehem to be the Saviour of all the world. Yet with all our joy, and the long centuries behind us of hearts made glad by His coming, we know there is much in us that deafens our ears to the sound of angel anthems, much that blinds us to the sight of guiding stars amid the darkness, much that crowds our hearts and minds, leaving little room for the humbler benedictions of this life. If repentance can purify our hope, if for this season we may become pure hearted, if now we can welcome you with all our soul, then grace us with your most wondrous blessing through Christ who was born to be the light of the world forever.

ANONYMOUS

Come, lovely Name!

Come, lovely Name; life of our hope!
Lo, we hold our hearts wide ope!
Unlock thy cabinet of day,
Dearest Sweet, and come away,
　Lo, how the thirsty lands
Gasp for thy golden showers, with long-stretched hands!
　Lo, how the labouring earth
　That hopes to be
　All heaven by thee,
　Leaps at thy birth! . . .

Come, royal Name; and pay the expense
Of all this precious patience;
　O come away,
And kill the death of this delay.
And see so many worlds of barren years
Melted and measured out in seas of tears.
O see the weary lids of wakeful hope
(Love's eastern windows) all wide ope
　With curtains drawn,
To catch the day-break of thy dawn.

RICHARD CRASHAW

Advent

I saw him with flesh all be-spread: He came from East.
I saw him with blood all be-shed: He came from West.
I saw that many he with him brought: He came from South.
I saw that the world of him ne rought: He came from North.

'I come from the wedlock as a sweet spouse that have my wife
    with me y-nome.
I come from fight as a stalwart knight that my foe have
    overcome.
I come from the cheaping as a rich chapman that mankind
    have y-bought.
I come from an uncouth land as a silly pilgrim that far have
    y-sought.'

ANONYMOUS

of him ne rought: cared nothing for him; y-nome: taken; cheaping: market; chapman:
merchant; uncouth: unknown; silly: simple

Christmas is coming . . .

There is no more dangerous or disgusting habit than that of celebrating Christmas before it comes, as I am doing in this article. It is the very essence of a festival that it breaks upon one brilliantly and abruptly, that at one moment the great day is not and the next moment the great day is. Up to a certain specific instant you are feeling ordinary and sad; for it is only Wednesday. At the next moment your heart leaps up and your soul and body dance together like lovers; for in one burst and blaze it has become Thursday. I am assuming (of course) that you are a worshipper of Thor, and that you celebrate his day once a week, possibly with human sacrifice. If, on the other hand, you are a modern Christian Englishman, you hail (of course) with the same explosion of gaity the appearance of the English Sunday. But I say that whatever the day is that is to you festive or symbolic, it is essential that there should be a quite clear black line between it and the time going before. And all the old wholesome customs in connection with Christmas were to the effect that one should not touch or see or know or speak of something before the actual coming of Christmas Day. Thus, for instance, children were never given their presents until the actual coming of the appointed hour. The presents were kept tied up in brown-paper parcels, out of which the arm of a doll or the leg of a donkey sometimes accidentally stuck. I wish this principle were adopted in respect of modern Christmas ceremonies and publications. Especially it ought to be observed in connection with what are called the Christmas numbers of magazines. The editors of the magazines bring out their Christmas numbers so long before the time that the reader is more likely to be still lamenting for the turkey of last year than to have seriously settled down to a solid anticipation of the turkey which is to come. Christmas numbers of magazines ought to be tied up in brown paper and kept for Christmas Day.

On consideration, I should favour the editors being tied up in brown paper. Whether the leg or arm of an editor should ever be allowed to protrude, I leave to individual choice.

G K CHESTERTON

The Illustrated London News, 29 December 1906

Preparations at Lulling

With only a fortnight to go before Christmas Day, Lulling people were beginning to bestir themselves about their shopping. London might start preparing for the festival at the end of October; Lulling refused to be hustled. October and November had jobs of their own in plenty. December, and the later part of that, was the proper time to think of Christmas, and the idea of buying cards and presents before then was just plain silly.

'Who wants to think of Christmas when there's the autumn digging to do?' said one practically.

'Takes all the gilt off the gingerbread to have Christmas thrown down your throat before December' agreed another.

But now all the good folk were ready for it, and the shops did a brisk trade. Baskets bulged, and harassed matrons struggled along the crowded main street bearing awkward objects like tricycles and pairs of stilts, flimsily wrapped in flapping paper. Children kept up a shrill piping for the tawdry knick-knacks which caught their eye, and fathers gazed speculatively at train sets and wondered if their two-year-old sons and daughters would be a good excuse to buy one.

At the corner of the Market Square stood Puddocks', the stationers, and here, one windy afternoon, Ella Bembridge was engaged in choosing Christmas cards.

Normally, Ella designed her own Christmas card. It was usually a wood cut or a lino cut, executed with her habitual vigour and very much appreciated by her friends. But somehow, this year, Ella had not done one. So many things had pressed upon her time. There were far more visits these days, both from the rector and from his friend Harold Shoesmith, and the vague unhappiness which hung over her at the thought of change had affected Ella more than she realized. Today, in Puddocks', reduced to turning over their mounds of insipid cards, Ella felt even more depressed.

But, depressed as she was, she set about her appointed task with energy. She made directly towards the section marked 'Cards 6d., 9d., and 1s.' and began a swift process of elimination. Ballet dancers, ponies, dogs, anyone in a crinoline or a beaver hat, were out. So were contrived scenes of an open Bible before a stained-glass window flanked with a Christmas rose or a candle. It was amazing how little was left after this ruthless pruning. Ella, coming up for air, looked at the throng around her to see how others were faring.

She envied the stout woman at her elbow who picked up all the cards embellished with sparkling stuff and read the verses intently. She had plenty of choice. She admired the way in which a tall thin man selected black and white line drawings of Ely Cathedral, Tower Bridge and Bath Abbey with extreme rapidity. She watched, with bitter respect, a large female who forced her way to the desk and demanded the ten dozen printed Christmas cards ordered on August 22nd, and promised faithfully for early December. Here was efficiency, thought Ella, returning to her rummaging.

MISS READ
Winter in Thrush Green

The Christmas Cards

Still it persists, the myth of snow
  at Christmas, Unashamedly across all our cards;
Not a few flakes but deep drifts –
Villages cosily half buried in it,
Trees, it would seem, gladly bearing
  its weight, Edwardian women wrapped in furs and skating,
Santa Claus showing us the story of the Father
For ever offering the marvellous unattainable gift,
Piercing a way through darkness to the hearth.

The Nativity may be ignored but new life is hoped for.
About this the cheap cards are surely right.
For white is everybody's secret emblem:
We half perceive the meaning of the virgin snow.

SISTER MARY LAURENCE

Christmas in the convent

I suppose the oddest thing that we do is not to go out to church. Our worship at Christmas, as every day, is in our own chapel within the convent. Apart from midnight mass, the pattern of our worship is the same as for the rest of the year. Vespers, compline, matins, terce, the eucharist, sext, and none punctuate every day, but the savour given by the plainsong distinguishes one season from another.

Advent has especially strong texts and melodies, building up to the Great O antiphons sung at vespers on the eight days before Christmas Eve: O Wisdom, O Dayspring, O Emmanuel . . . Come! Come and save us, show the light of your countenance and we shall be whole. Each prays this for herself first and last, and we pray it with and for our brothers and sisters, known and unknown, and especially for any who may be too busy or troubled to bring this hope and longing to their lips.

Our Christmas starts late by the world's reckoning: not until Christmas Eve do we decorate the tree and set up the crib in the chapel, listening to the broadcast of Nine Lessons and Carols. The time for silent prayer between that and the evening service of vespers has a special quality. Even in a convent, it can be hard to stop putting the finishing touch, rewriting that list, checking whether everything is ready for the next meal. But the most restless of us is drawn to be still and wait in the last hour of Advent.

Midnight mass — plainsong like our Sunday and feast-day Eucharists — has for some of us a particular poignancy. Until quite recently we would gather each morning at 2 a.m. for the office of matins (though not by any means all of us). Fewer and fewer sisters were able to sustain this rhythm of sleeping and waking (and sleeping again, if you were blessed). Changing to an early-morning matins was a hard decision: it felt like abandoning something that had been entrusted to us — the choice to make our bleary way to chapel while the world slept or partied or suffered.

But tonight our song is 'Glory to God in the highest' and 'Let the heavens be joyful, and let the earth rejoice in the presence of the Lord, for he is come'.

SR CATHERINE AND SR CLARE-LOUISE SLG

Snow in Bethlehem

This is written amid fields of snow within a few days of Christmas. And when last I saw snow it was within a few miles of Bethlehem. The coincidence will serve as a symbol of something I have noticed all my life, though it is not very easy to sum up. It is generally the romantic thing that turns out to be the real thing, under the extreme test of realism. It is the sceptical and even rational legend that turns out to be entirely legendary. Everything I had been taught or told led me to regard snow in Bethlehem as a paradox, like snow in Egypt. Every rumour of realism, every indirect form of rationalism, every scientific opinion taken on authority and at third hand, had led me to regard the country where Christ was born solely as a sort of semi-tropical place with nothing but palm-trees and parasols. It was only when I actually looked at it that it looked exactly like a Christmas card.

G K CHESTERTON
The Illustrated London News, 1920

Preparing for Christmas

The Christmas season is domestic; and for that reason most people now prepare for it by struggling in tramcars, standing in queues, rushing away in trains, crowding despairingly into tea-shops, and wondering when or whether they will ever get home. I do not know whether some of them disappear for ever in the toy department or simply lie down and die in the tea-rooms; but by the look of them, it is quite likely. Just before the great festival of the home the whole population seems to have become homeless. It is the supreme triumph of industrial civilisation that, in the huge cities which seem to have far too many houses, there is a hopeless shortage of housing. For a long time past great numbers of our poor have become practically nomadic. We even confess the fact; for we talk of them as Street Arabs. But this domestic institution, in its present ironical phase, has gone beyond such normal abnormality. The feast of the family turns the rich as well as the poor into vagabonds. They are so scattered over the bewildering labyrinth of our traffic and our trade, that they sometimes cannot even reach the tea-shop; it would be indelicate, of course, to mention the tavern. They have a difficulty in crowding into their hotels, let alone separating to reach their houses. I mean quite the reverse of irreverence when I say that their only point of resemblance to the archetypal Christmas family is that there is no room for them at the inn.

G K CHESTERTON
The Thing

Advent Carol

If ye would hear the angels sing
  'Peace on earth and mercy mild',
  Think of him who was once a child,
On Christmas Day in the morning.

If ye would hear the angels sing,
  Rise, and spread your Christmas fare;
  'Tis merrier still the more that share,
On Christmas Day in the morning.

Rise, and bake your Christmas bread;
  Christians, rise! the world is bare,
  And blank, and dark with want and care,
Yet Christmas comes in the morning.

If ye would hear the angels sing,
  Rise, and light your Christmas fire;
  And see that ye pile the logs still higher
On Christmas Day in the morning.

Rise, and light your Christmas fire;
  Christians, rise! the world is old,
  And Time is weary, and worn, and cold,
Yet Christmas comes in the morning.

If ye would hear the angels sing,
  Christians! see ye let each door
  Stand wider than it e'er stood before,
On Christmas Day in the morning.

Rise, and open wide the door;
  Christians, rise! the world is wide,
  And many there be that stand outside,
Yet Christmas comes in the morning.

DORA GREENWELL

On Christmas Presents

A little while ago I saw a statement by Mrs Eddy [Mary Baker Eddy, the founder of Christian Science] on this subject, in which she said that she did not give presents in a gross, sensuous, terrestrial sense, but sat still and thought about Truth and Purity till all her friends were much better for it. Now I do not say that this plan is either superstitious or impossible, and no doubt it has an economic charm. I say it is un-Christian in the same solid and prosaic sense that playing a tune backwards is unmusical or saying 'ain't' is ungrammatical. I do not know that there is any Scriptural text or Church Council that condemns Mrs Eddy's theory of Christmas presents: but Christianity condemns it, as soldiering condemns running away. The two attitudes are antagonistic not only in their theology, not only in their thought, but in their state of soul before they ever begin to think. The idea of embodying goodwill – that is, of putting it into a body – is the huge and primal idea of the Incarnation. A gift of God that can be seen and touched is the whole point of the epigram of the creed. Christ Himself was a Christmas present. The note of material Christmas presents is struck even before He is born in the first movements of the sages and the star. The Three Kings came to Bethlehem bringing gold and frankincense and myrrh. If they had only brought Truth and Purity and Love there would have been no Christian art and no Christian civilisation . . .

G K CHESTERTON
The Theology of Christmas Presents

***

Christmas presents are a standing protest on behalf of giving as distinct from that mere sharing that modern moralists offer as equivalent or superior. Christmas stands for this superb and sacred paradox: that it is a higher spiritual transaction for

Tommy and Molly each to give each other sixpence than for both equally to share a shilling. Christmas is something better than a thing for all; it is a thing for everybody. And if anyone finds such phrases aimless or fantastic, or thinks that the distinction has no existence except in a refinement of words, the only test is that I have indicated already – the permanent test of the populace. Take any hundred girls from a board school and see whether they do not make a distinction between a flower for each and a garden for all. If therefore new spiritual schools are concerned to prove that they have the spirit and secret of the Christian festival, they must prove it, not by abstract affirmations, but by things that have a special and unmistakable smack, by hitting one pungent tinge of taste, by being able to write a Christmas carol, or even to make a Christmas pie.

G K CHESTERTON
The Contemporary Review, January 1910

Christmas for Animals

Advent preparations are not simply to be confined to our fellow men and women. St Francis of Assisi would often say:

If I were to speak to the Emperor, I would, supplicating and persuading him tell him for the love of God and me to make a special law that no man should take or kill sister Larks, nor do them any harm. Likewise, that all the Podestas of the towns, and the Lords of castles and villages, should be bound every year on Christmas day to compel men to throw wheat and other grains outside the cities and castles, that our sister Larks may have something to eat, and also the other birds, on a day of such solemnity.

And that for the reverence of the Son of God, Who rested on that night with the most blessed Virgin Mary between an Ox and an Ass, they shall be bound to provide for them on that night the best of good fodder. Likewise on that day, all poor men should be satisfied by the rich with good food. For the blessed Father had a greater reverence for Christmas day than for any other festival, saying, 'Since the Lord had been born for us, it behoves us to be saved,' and on account of which he wished that on that day every Christian should rejoice in the Lord; and for His love who gave Himself for us, that all should provide largely not only for the poor, but also for the animals and birds.

The Mirror of Perfection

The Reminder

While I watch the Christmas blaze
Paint the room with ruddy rays,
Something makes my vision glide
To the frosty scene outside.

There, to reach a rotting berry,
Toils a thrush – constrained to very
Dregs of food by sharp distress,
Taking such with thankfulness.

Why, O starving bird, when I
One day's joy would justify,
And put misery out of view,
Do you make me notice you?

THOMAS HARDY

The Crib

They are making a crèche at the Saturday morning classes
For the Christmas party: scissors and paper vie
With fingers and plasticine until there are masses
Of sheep and shepherds that kneel and stand and lie,

And cotton-batting angels with cellophane wings
And a golden cardboard star and string to guide it
And pipe-cleaner camels carrying tin-foil kings
And a real straw manger with Joseph and Mary beside it.

But the manger is empty. The Saturday classes contain
So many different faiths, there is a danger
Of giving offence; there was once no room in the inn,
Now there is no room for him in the manger.

Of course he will understand, his love is hearty
Enough to forgive and forget the being slighted
And true enough not to offend at the birthday party
By showing up where he is uninvited.

Besides he is long accustomed to the manners
Of centuries that consecrate the snub
Of Christmas honoured, not the one it honours.
Strange they should trouble to give the crèche a crib.

ROBERT FINCH

The First Christmas Crib at Greccio

It is an irony that the first crib, made by St Francis to show the villagers at Greccio the shocking, grim realities of birth in a stable, has grown into a familiar, expected institution. From the guildpageants to the Sunday School children's nativity play, and in every medium from wood, china, cardboard to plaster-of-paris, we see the still centre of the Christmas story – the baby Jesus lying in the manger at Bethlehem. Some scholars now believe that Luke's gospel account is poetry – written to teach us something about Christ's birth, but not a historical account of what happened. If we let this shake our faith, we are looking for the wrong assurances. Francis – being both a poet and a mystic – saw straight to the heart of the story. He saw the beauty and helplessness of a human baby set against the squalid conditions of the stable; the presence of the animals, waiting like us for their king; the dramatic contrast between the poverty of the stable and the richness of God's love.

Now three years before his death it befell that he [St Francis] was minded, at the town of Greccio, to celebrate the memory of the Birth of the Child Jesus, with all the added solemnity that he might, for the kindling of devotion. That his might not seem an innovation, he sought and obtained licence from the Supreme Pontiff, and then made ready a manger, and bade hay, together with an ox and an ass, be brought unto the spot. The Brethren were called together, the folk assembled, the wood echoed with their voices, and that august night was made radiant and solemn with many bright lights, and with tuneful and sonorous praises. The man of God, filled with tender love, stood before the manger, bathed in tears, and overflowing with joy. Solemn Masses were celebrated over the manger, Francis, the Levite of Christ, chanting the Holy Gospel. Then he preached unto the folk standing round of the Birth of the King in poverty, calling Him, when he wished to name Him, the Child of Bethlehem, by reason of his tender love for Him.

A certain knight, valorous and true, Messer John of Greccio, who for the love of Christ had left the secular army, and was bound by closest friendship unto the man of God, declared that he beheld a little Child right fair to see sleeping in that manger, Who seemed to be awakened from sleep when the blessed Father Francis embraced Him in both arms. This vision of the devout knight is rendered worth of belief, not alone through the holiness of him that beheld it, but is also confirmed by the truth that it set forth, and withal proven by the miracles that followed it. For the ensample of Francis, if meditated upon by the world, must needs stir up sluggish hearts unto the faith of Christ, and the hay that was kept back from the manger by the folk proved a marvellous remedy for sick beasts, and a prophylactic against divers other plagues, God magnifying by all means His servant, and making manifest by clear and miraculous portents the efficacy of his powers.

ST BONAVENTURE
The Life of St Francis

A Christmas Letter from Germany

There is a Christmas custom here which pleased and interested me. The children make little presents to their parents, and to each other, and the parents to their children. For three or four months before Christmas the girls are all busy, and the boys save up their pocket money to buy these presents. What the present is to be is cautiously kept secret; and the girls have a world of contrivances to conceal it – such as working when they are out on visits, and the others are not with them, getting up in the morning before daylight, etc. Then on the evening before Christmas Day, one of the parlours is lighted up by the children, into which the parents must not go; a great yew bough is fastened on the table at a little distance from the wall, a multitude of little tapers are fixed in the bough, but not so as to burn it till they are nearly consumed, and coloured paper, etc., hangs and flutters from the twigs. Under this bough the children lay out in great order the presents they mean for their parents, still concealing in the pockets what they intend for each other. Then the parents are introduced, and each presents his little gift; they then bring out the remainder one by one from their pockets, and present them with kisses and embraces. Where I witnessed this scene there were eight or nine children, and the eldest daughter and the mother wept aloud for joy and tenderness; and the tears ran down the face of the father, and he clasped all his children so tight to his breast, it seemed as if he did it to stifle the sob that was rising within it. I was very much affected . . .

SAMUEL TAYLOR COLERIDGE

Hospitality for the Homeless

The Traveller comes across an ancient charity inscribed over a little old door as he wanders about the old Cathedral city of Rochester, one Christmas Eve:

RICHARD WATTS, Esq.
by his Will, dated 22 Aug. 1579,
founded this Charity
for Six poor Travellers,
who not being ROGUES, or PROCTORS,
May receive gratis for one Night,
Lodging, Entertainment,
and Fourpence each.

Knowing that he is not a Proctor, and hoping that he is not a Rogue, the Traveller decides to claim his due...

I found it to be a clean white house, of a staid and venerable air, with the quaint old door already three times mentioned [an arched door], choice little long low lattice-windows, and a roof of three gables...I was very well pleased, both with my property and its situation. While I was yet surveying it with growing content, I espied, at one of the upper lattices which stood open, a decent body, of a wholesome matronly appearance, whose eyes I caught enquiringly addressed to mine. They said so plainly, 'Do you wish to see the houses?' that I answered aloud, 'Yes, if you please.' And within a minute the old door opened, and I bent my head, and went down two steps into the entry.

'This,' said the matronly presence, ushering me into a low room on the right, 'is where the Travellers sit by the fire, and cook what bits of suppers they buy with their fourpences.'

'O! Then they have no Entertainment?' said I. For the inscription over the outer door was still running in my head, and I was mentally repeating, in a kind of tune, 'Lodging, entertainment, and fourpence each.'

'They have a fire provided for 'em,' returned the matron, – a mighty civil person, not, as I could make out, overpaid; 'and these cooking utensils. And this what's painted on a board is the rules for their behaviour. They have their fourpences when they get their tickets from the steward over the way – for I don't admit 'em myself, they must get their tickets first – and sometimes one buys a rasher of bacon, and another a herring, and another a pound of potatoes, or what not. Sometimes two or three of 'em will club their fourpences together, and make a supper that way. But not much of anything is to be got for fourpence, at present, when provisions is so dear.'

'True indeed,' I remarked. I had been looking about the room, admiring its snug fire-side at the upper end, its glimpse of the street through the low mullioned window, and its beams overhead. 'It is very comfortable,' said I.

'Ill-conwenient,' observed the matronly presence.

I liked to hear her say so; for it showed a commendable anxiety to execute in no niggardly spirit the intentions of Master Richard Watts. But the room was really so well adapted to its purpose that I protested, quite enthusiastically, against her disparagement.

'Nay, ma'am,' said I. 'I am sure it is warm in winter and cool in summer. It has a look of homely welcome and soothing rest. It has a remarkably cosy fireside, the very blink of which, gleaming out into the street upon a winter night, is enough to warm all Rochester's heart. And as to the convenience of the six Poor Travellers – .'

'I don't mean them,' returned the presence. 'I speak of its being an ill-conwenience to myself and my daughter, having no other room to sit in of a night.'

This was true enough, but there was another quaint room of corresponding dimensions on the opposite side of the entry: so I stepped across to it, through the open doors of both rooms, and asked what this chamber was for.

'This,' returned the presence, 'is the Board Room. Where the gentlemen meet when they come here.'

Let me see. I had counted from the street six upper windows besides these on the ground-story. Making a perplexed calculation in my mind, I rejoined, 'Then the six Poor Travellers sleep up-stairs?'

My new friend shook her head. 'They sleep,' she answered, 'in two little outer galleries at the back, where their beds has always been, ever since the Charity was founded. It being so very ill-conwenient to me as things is at present, the gentlemen are going to take off a bit of the back-yard, and make a slip of a room for 'em three, to sit in before they go to bed.'

'And then the six Poor Travellers,' said I, 'will be entirely out of the house?'

'Entirely out of the house,' assented the presence, comfortably smoothing her hands. 'Which is considered much better for all parties, and much more conwenient.'

I had been a little startled, in the Cathedral, by the emphasis with which the effigy of Master Richard Watts was bursting out of his tomb; but I began to think, now, that it might be expected to come across the High-street some stormy night, and make a disturbance here.

* * *

'And pray, ma'am,' said I, sensible that the blankness of my face began to brighten as the thought occurred to me, 'could one see these Travellers?'

'Well!' she returned dubiously, 'no!'

'Not tonight, for instance?' said I.

'Well!' she returned more positively, 'no. Nobody ever asked to see them, and nobody ever did see them.'

As I am not easily balked in a design when I am set upon it, I urged to the good lady that this was Christmas Eve; that Christmas comes but once a year – which is unhappily too true, for when it begins to stay with us the whole year round we shall make this earth a very different place; that I was possessed by the desire to treat the Travellers to a supper and a temperate glass of hot Wassail; that the voice of Fame had been heard in

26

that land, declaring my ability to make hot Wassail; that if I were permitted to hold the feast, I should be found conformable to reason, sobriety, and good hours; in a word, that I could be merry and wise myself, and had been even known at a pinch to keep others so, although I was decorated with no badge or medal, and was not a Brother, Orator, Apostle, Saint, or Prophet of any denomination whatever. In the end I prevailed, to my great joy. It was settled that at nine o'clock that night a Turkey and a piece of Roast Beef should smoke upon the board; and that I, faint and unworthy minister for once of Master Richard Watts, should preside as the Christmas-supper host of the six Poor Travellers.

I went back to my inn to give the necessary directions for the Turkey and Roast Beef, and, during the remainder of the day, could settle to nothing for thinking of the Poor Travellers. When the wind blew hard against the windows, – it was a cold day, with dark gusts of sleet alternating with periods of wild brightness, as if the year were dying fitfully, – I pictured them advancing towards their resting-place along various cold roads, and felt delighted to think how little they foresaw the supper that awaited them. I painted their portraits in my mind, and indulged in little heightening touches. I made them footsore; I made them weary; I made them carry packs and bundles; I made them stop by finger-posts and milestones, leaning on their bent sticks, and looking wistfully at what was written there; I made them lose their way; and filled their five wits with apprehensions of lying out all night, and being frozen to death. I took up my hat, and went out, climbed to the top of the Old Castle, and looked over the windy hills that slope down to the Medway, almost believing that I could descry some of my Travellers in the distance. After it fell dark, and the Cathedral bell was heard in the invisible steeple – quite a bower of frosty rime when I had last seen it –striking five, six, seven, I became so full of my Travellers that I could eat no dinner, and felt constrained to watch them still in the red coals of my fire.

The Travellers were all assembled, the cloth was laid... I found the party to be thus composed. Firstly, myself. Secondly, a very decent man indeed, with his right arm in a sling, who had a certain clean agreeable smell of wood about him, from which I judged him to have something to do with shipbuilding. Thirdly, a little sailor-boy, a mere child, with a profusion of rich dark brown hair, and deep womanly-looking eyes. Fourthly, a shabby-genteel personage in a threadbare black suit, and apparently in very bad circumstances, with a dry suspicious look; the absent buttons on his waistcoat eked out with red tape; and a bundle of extraordinarily tattered papers sticking out of an inner breast-pocket. Fifthly, a foreigner by birth, but an Englishman in speech, who carried his pipe in the band of his hat, and lost no time in telling me, in an easy, simple, engaging way, that he was a watchmaker from Geneva, and travelled all about the Continent, mostly on foot, working as a journeyman, and seeing new countries, – possibly (I thought) also smuggling a watch or so, now and then. Sixthly, a little widow, who had been very pretty and was still very young, but whose beauty had been wrecked in some great misfortune, and whose manner was remarkably timid, scared, and solitary. Seventhly and lastly, a Traveller of a kind familiar to my boyhood, but now almost obsolete, – a Book-Pedler, who had a quantity of Pamphlets and Numbers with him, and who presently boasted that he could repeat more verses in an evening than he could sell in a twelvemonth ... It made my heart rejoice to observe how their wind and frost hardened faces softened in the clatter of plates and knives and forks, and mellowed in the fire and supper heat. While their hats and caps and wrappers, hanging up, a few small bundles on the ground in a corner, and in another corner three or four old walking sticks, worn down at the end to a mere fringe, linked this snug interior with the bleak outside in a golden chain.

CHARLES DICKENS
Christmas Stories

Noblesse Oblige

Sara Crewe, the fabulously rich 'little princess' has been orphaned and abandoned to the cruel mercies of Mrs Minchin. Living in the same square is a large, happy family whom Sara secretly watches with longing and affection, giving them romantic names and stories.

One evening a very funny thing happened – though, perhaps, in one sense it was not a funny thing at all.

Several of the Montmorencys were evidently going to a children's party, and just as Sara was about to pass the door they were crossing the pavement to get into the carriage which was waiting for them. Veronica Eustacia and Rosalind Gladys, in white lace frocks and lovely sashes, had just got in, and Guy Clarence, aged five, was following them. He was such a pretty fellow and had such a darling little round head covered with curls, that Sara forgot her basket and shabby cloak altogether – in fact, forgot everything but that she wanted to look at him for a moment. So she paused and looked.

It was Christmas time, and the Large Family had been hearing many stories about children who were poor and had no mammas and papas to fill their stockings and take them to the pantomime – children who were, in fact, cold and thinly clad and hungry. In the stories, kind people – sometimes little boys and girls with tender hearts – invariably saw the poor children and gave them money or rich gifts, or took them home to beautiful dinners. Guy Clarence had been affected to tears that very afternoon by the reading of such a story, and he had burned with desire to find such a poor child and give her a certain sixpence he possessed, and thus provide for her for life. An entire sixpence, he was sure, would mean affluence for evermore. As he crossed the strip of red carpet laid across the pavement from the door to the carriage, he had this very sixpence in the pocket of his very short man-o'-war trousers. And just as Rosalind Gladys got into the vehicle and jumped on to the seat in order to feel the cushions spring under her, he saw Sara standing on the wet pavement in her shabby frock and hat, with her old basket on her arm, looking at him hungrily.

He thought that her eyes looked hungry because she perhaps had nothing to eat for a long time. He did not know that they looked so because she was hungry for the warm, merry life his home held and his rosy face spoke of, and that she had a hungry wish to snatch him in her arms and kiss him. He only knew that she had big eyes and a thin face and thin legs, and a common basket and poor clothes. So he put his hand in his pocket and found his sixpence, and walked up to her benignly.

'Here, poor little girl,' he said. 'Here is a sixpence. I will give it to you.'

Sara started, and all at once realized that she looked exactly like poor children she had seen, in her better days, waiting on the pavement to watch her as she got out of her brougham. And she had given them pennies many a time. Her face went red and then it went pale, and for a second she felt as if she could not take the dear little sixpence.

'Oh, no!' she said. 'Oh no, thank you; I mustn't take it, indeed!'

Her voice was so unlike an ordinary street child's voice, and her manner was so like the manner of a well-bred little person that Veronica Eustacia (whose real name was Janet) and Rosalind Gladys (who was really called Nora) leaned forward to listen.

But Guy Clarence was not to be thwarted in his benevolence. He thrust the sixpence into her hand.

'Yes, you must take it, poor girl!' he insisted stoutly. 'You can buy things to eat with it. It is a whole sixpence!'

There was something so honest and kind in his face, and he looked so likely to be heartbrokenly disappointed if she did not take it, that Sara knew that she must not refuse him. To be as proud as that would be a cruel thing. So she actually put her pride in her pocket, though it must be admitted her cheeks burned.

'Thank you,' she said. 'You are a kind, kind little darling thing.' And as he scrambled joyfully into the carriage she went away, trying to smile, though she caught her breath quickly and her eyes were shining through a mist. She had known that she looked odd and shabby, but until now she had not known that she might be taken for a beggar.

FRANCES HODGSON BURNETT
A Little Princess

Christmas Day in the Workhouse

It is Christmas Day in the Workhouse,
  And the cold bare walls are bright
With garlands of green and holly,
  And the place is a pleasant sight:
For with clean-washed hands and faces,
  In a long and hungry line
The paupers sit at the tables,
  For this is the hour they dine.

And the guardians and their ladies,
  Although the wind is east
Have come in their furs and wrappers,
  To watch their charges feast;
To smile and be condescending,
  Put pudding on pauper plates,
To be hosts at the workhouse banquet
  They've paid for – with the rates.

Oh, the paupers are meek and lowly
  With their 'Thank'ee kindly, mum's';
So long as they fill their stomachs,
  What matter it whence it comes?
But one of the old men mutters,
  And pushes his plate aside:
'Great God!' he cries; 'but it chokes me!
  For this is the day *she* died.'

The guardians gazed in horror;
  The master's face went white;
'Did a pauper refuse their pudding?'
  Could their eyes believe aright?
Then the ladies clutched their husbands,
  Thinking the man would die,

Struck by a bolt, or something,
  By the outraged One on high.

But the pauper sat for a moment,
  Then rose 'mid a silence grim.
For the others had ceased to chatter,
  And trembled in every limb.
He looked at the guardians' ladies,
  Then, eyeing their lords, he said,
'I eat not the food of villains
  Whose hands are foul and red:

'Whose victims cry for vengeance
  From their dank, unhallowed graves.'
'He's drunk!' said the workhouse master,
  'Or else he's mad, and raves.'
'Not drunk, or mad,' cried the pauper,
  'But only a haunted beast,
Who, torn by the hounds and mangled,
  Declines the vulture's feast.

'I care not a curse for the guardians,
  And I won't be dragged away.
Just let me have the fit out.
  It's only on Christmas Day
That the black past comes to goad me,
  And prey on my burning brain;
I'll tell you the rest in a whisper, –
  I swear I won't shout again.

'Keep your hands off me, curse you!
  Hear me right out to the end.
You come here to see how the paupers
  The season of Christmas spend.
You come here to watch us feeding,
  As they watch the captured beast.
Hear why a penniless pauper
  Spits on your paltry feast.

'Do you think I will take your bounty,
   And let you smile and think
You're doing a noble action
   With the parish's meat and drink?
Where is my wife, you traitors –
   The poor old wife you slew?
Yes, by the God above us,
   My Nance was killed by you!

'Last winter my wife lay dying,
   Starved in a filthy den;
I had never been to the parish, –
   I came to the parish then.
I swallowed my pride in coming,
   For, ere the ruin came,
I held up my head as a trader,
   And I bore a spotless name.

'I came to the parish, craving
   Bread for a starving wife,
Bread for the woman who'd loved me
   Through fifty years of life;
And what do you think they told me,
   Mocking my awful grief?
That "the House" was open to us,
   But they wouldn't give "out relief".

'I slunk to the filthy alley –
   'Twas a cold, raw Christmas eve –
And the bakers' shops were open,
   Tempting a man to thieve;
But I clenched my fists together,
   Holding my head awry,
So I came to her empty-handed,
   And mournfully told her why.

'Then I told her, "the House" was open;
   She had heard of the ways of that,
For her bloodless cheeks went crimson,

34

And up in her rags she sat,
Crying, "Bide the Christmas here, John,
    We've never had one apart;
I think I can bear the hunger, -
    The other would break my heart."

'All through that eve I watched her,
    Holding her hand in mine,
Praying the Lord, and weeping
    Till my lips were salt as brine,
I asked her once if she hungered,
    And as she answered "No,"
The moon shone in at the window
    Set in a wreath of snow.

'Then the room was bathed in glory,
    And I saw in my darling's eyes
The far-away look of wonder
    That comes when the spirit flies;
And her lips were parched and parted,
    And her reason came and went,
For she raved of our home in Devon
    Where our happiest years were spent.

'And the accents, long forgotten,
    Came back to the tongue once more,
For she talked like the country lassie
    I woo'd by the Devon shore,
Then she rose to her feet and trembled,
    And fell on the rags and moaned,
And, "Give me a crust – I'm famished –
    For the love of God!" she groaned.

'I rushed from the room like a madman,
    And flew to the workhouse gate.
Crying, "Food for a dying woman!"
    And the answer came, "Too late."
They drove me away with curses;
    Then I fought with a dog in the street,

And tore from the mongrel's clutches
  A crust he was trying to eat.

'Back, through the filthy by-lanes!
  Back, through the trampled slush!
Up to the crazy garret,
  Wrapped in an awful hush.
My heart sank down at the threshold,
  And I paused with a sudden thrill,
For there in the silv'ry moonlight
  My Nance lay, cold and still.

'Up to the blackened ceiling
  The sunken eyes were cast –
I knew on those lips all bloodless
  My name had been the last;
She'd called for her absent husband –
  O God! had I but known! –
Had called in vain, and in anguish
  Had died in that den – *alone*.

'Yes, there, in a land of plenty,
  Lay a loving woman dead,
Cruelly starved and murdered
  For a loaf of the parish bread.
At yonder gate, last Christmas,
  I craved for a human life.
You, who would feast us paupers,
  What of my murdered wife!

'There, get ye gone to your dinners;
  Don't mind me in the least;
Think of the happy paupers
  Eating your Christmas feast;
And when you recount their blessings
  In your smug parochial way,
Say what you did for *me*, too,
  Only last Christmas Day.'

GEORGE SIMS

The House of Christmas

There fared a mother driven forth,
Out of an inn to roam;
In the place where she was homeless
All men are at home.
The crazy stable close at hand,
With shaking timber and shifting sand,
Grew a stronger thing to abide and stand
Than the square stones of Rome.

For men are homesick in their homes,
And strangers under the sun,
And they lay their heads in a foreign land
Whenever the day is done.
Here we have battle and blazing eyes
And chance and honour and high surprise,
But our homes are under miraculous skies
Where the yule tale was begun.

A child in a foul stable,
Where the beasts feed and foam;
Only where he was homeless
Are you and I at home;
We have hands that fashion and heads that know,
But our hearts we lost – how long ago!
In a place no chart nor ship can show
Under the sky's dome.

This world is wild as an old wives' tale,
And strange the plain things are,
The earth is enough and the air is enough
For our wonder and our war;
But our rest is as far as the fire-drake swings
And our peace is put in impossible things

Where clashed and thundered unthinkable wings
Round an incredible star.

To an open house in the evening
Home shall all men come,
To an older place than Eden
And a taller town than Rome.
To the end of the way of the wandering star,
To the things that cannot be and that are,
To the place where God was homeless
And all men are at home.

G K CHESTERTON

Nativity

The King is Coming

Yet if His Majesty, our sovereign Lord,
Should of his own accord
Friendly himself invite,
And say 'I'll be your guest to-morrow night,'
How should we stir ourselves, call and command
All hands to work! 'Let no man idle stand!
'Set me fine Spanish tables in the hall;
See they be fitted all;
Let there be room to eat
And order taken that there want no meat.
See every sconce and candlestick made bright,
That without tapers they may give a light.
'Look to the presence; are the carpets spread,
The dazie o'er the head,
The cushions in the chairs,
And all the candles lighted on the stairs?
Perfume the chambers, and in any case
Let each man give attendance in his place!'
Thus, if a king were coming, would we do;
And 'twere good reason too;
For 'tis a duteous thing
To show all honour to an earthly king,
And after all our travail and our cost
So he be pleased, to think no labour lost.

But at the coming of the King of heaven
All's set at six and seven;
We wallow in our sin,
Christ cannot find a chamber in the inn.
We entertain Him always like a stranger,
And, as at first, still lodge Him in the manger.

ANONYMOUS

Christmas

All after pleasures as I rode one day,
　My horse and I, both tired, body and mind,
With full cry of affections, quite astray,
　I took up in the next inn I could find.

There when I came, whom found I but my dear,
　My dearest Lord, expecting till the grief
Of pleasures brought me to Him, ready there
　To be all passengers' sweet relief.

O Thou, Whose glorious yet contracted light,
　Wrapped in Night's mantle, stole into a manger,
Since my dark soul and brutish, is Thy right,
　To man, of all beasts, be not Thou a stranger:

Furnish and deck my soul, that Thou mayst have
A better lodging than a rack or grave.

GEORGE HERBERT

No Room

No room at the Holiday Inn;
No room in the holiday for them!
'Two hots and a cot' at the 'Army'
And a cardboard box
   over a sewer grate
   Is 'home' and a 'central heat'.

And they shall be called
   'shopping bag ladies',
   'street people',
   'the homeless'.

They know about
   giving birth on the run
   and keeping on the move
   to stay alive.
Smelly places of birth
   and lonely places of death
   are more than
     Bible stories to them.

They peer into the window
   of my soul;
   decorated as it is
   with Christmas lights
   and presents under the tree.
And I gaze out into the dark:
   the night in which
   an anonymous Joseph and Mary
   seek a place in my world
   for love to be born.

No room in the Holiday Inn;
   not even room in the holiday
   for love to be born. Alas!

CORNELIUS KANHAI

Christmas begins with laughter

Actually, the Christmas story begins with laughter. Wrapped up inside this laughter is an intense nervousness. The sensation of joy that erupts from some profound place within also sounds an unmistakable note of amazement. 'Surely this can't really be happening to me' But it is. You are the one who has been chosen.

The laughter that begins this story comes from Sara, the wife of Abraham the patriarch. She cannot believe her eyes or her ears. The vision of strangely angelic visitors seated in her nomad's encampment at Mamre was dream-like. The consequent prediction that even in old age, she could yet have the child she longed for was laughable. So Sara laughed.

Her laughter has been remembered by subsequent generations because Sara did have a child, Isaac. God's promise to her was fulfilled, and the expectation that the unimaginable can really happen was planted in human minds as a definitive characteristic of how we encounter the divine love.

At some point in the darkness of the night of Christmas Eve, the story that begins with Sara's laughter takes a decisive new twist. Time and eternity intersect; earth unites with heaven; humanity is reconciled with God. It is all an astonishing marriage, universal and eternal in its scope.

The roll call of shepherds, innkeeper, Joseph, the Virgin Mary, and the baby Jesus, with no room at the inn, is so familiar that we have to work hard to recover our sense of astonishment at what is happening. Perhaps we need a little of Sara's laughter, a renewed apprehension that this marriage event is serious, real, terrifyingly beautiful, and we cannot escape its implications.

Like the birth of Isaac, there is something miraculous about the birth of Jesus. Mary expresses amazement similar to Sara's: 'How can this be?' (Luke 1.34) We get close to something like laughter when Mary and her cousin Elizabeth get together before Jesus is born and have a raucous celebration, described by the same word that is used for King David's triumphal entry with the Ark into Jerusalem (Luke 1.41).

The new twist in the story is two-fold. First, the unseen God, known only in visions and dreams, is now seen in the human fragility of the Christ-child. This is the force of St John's unfolding of the mystery of the incarnation: 'the word was made flesh and dwelt among us' (John 1.14).

Secondly, the covenant relationship established with the descendents of Abraham and Sara now reaches maturity, and becomes the foundation of hope and peace for all people. This is the good news of the angels' message: 'Glory to God in the highest heaven, and on earth peace' (Luke 1.14).

If the full implication of this is difficult for us to take in, we can perhaps get closer to it through the human experience and language of marriage. Year after year, the Church of England prepares thousands of people for marriage, and hosts the celebration of their wedding service.

Sacred words are given to bride and groom to say to each other. These words sum up what we believe the gift of marriage to be, and they are astonishing in their scope. Some of them also sum up what we believe is happening at Christmas.

"All that I am I give to you, and all that I have I share with you," say bride and groom when they exchange rings. We could equally say these words as we give to God the one thing that God does not have; the mortal frailty of human life.

All this that we are and have, our limitations and frailty, we give to God, who takes flesh in the womb of Mary, and is born as one like us. In exchange, God reveals to us that the life of heaven, divinity itself, symbolised by the return to paradise — this is the scope of the divine self-giving, when on Christmas night earth is wedded to heaven.

MARTIN WARNER

Unnailing Christmas

Of the two Christmas sermons I have heard recently, one seemed to be saying that Christ came to earth so that I could join an enquirers' group, while the other understood it as an education in the evils of homelessness.

We are compulsive finders of meaning. Like those who pin down moths, we like to pin down events with explanation. Whether in our personal, religious, or national histories, we love 'decisive events' after which 'nothing was the same again'. So whether it is a personal experience or a painting by Cézanne, we feel happy when we can say with Julian: 'This was its meaning.'

Of course, no event has less than a thousand meanings; but we tend to ignore the 999 and claim sovereignty for a random one.

These things are not surprising, since for many of us, such organisation of events serves to calm a primal terror. The pursuit of meaning is a child's cry from the heart in a frightening universe — and who would not want to attend to that cry? Particularly at Christmas, a festival with so many hopes and fears. The temptation, in the language of *The X Factor* judges, is to 'nail it'.

But perhaps Christmas is best left unnailed; best left as Great Story rather than Desperate Explanation. Indeed, instead of feeling they must find Christmas, the daring will allow Christmas to find them, as it once did me.

When I worked in a supermarket, the misnamed festive season presented its own challenges. When the "gripe and grab" of the turbulent shop-floor got too much, I would sometimes withdraw for a while to the store warehouse, a more peaceful sanctuary than most cathedrals these days. And there, in the stillness of crate and box, each waiting to be opened, I got as close to the manger as I ever have.

Downstairs, the tills went 'Kerching!', but away in a warehouse, a surprising Christmas found me; a retail redemption.

SIMON PARKE

The Carol Singers of Mellstock

The older men and musicians wore thick coats, with stiff perpendicular collars, and coloured handkerchiefs wound round and round the neck till the end came to hand, over all which they just showed their ears and noses, like people looking over a wall. The remainder, stalwart ruddy men and boys, were dressed mainly in snow-white smock-frocks, embroidered upon the shoulders and breasts in ornamental forms of hearts, diamonds, and zigzags. The cider-mug was emptied for the ninth time, the music-books were arranged, and the pieces finally decided upon. The boys in the meantime put the old horn-lanterns in order, cut candles into short lengths to fit the lanterns; and, a thin fleece of snow having fallen since the early part of the evening, those who had no leggings went to the stable and wound wisps of hay round their ankles to keep the insidious flakes from the interior of their boots . . .

Just before the clock struck twelve they lighted the lanterns and started. The moon, in her third quarter, had risen since the snow-storm; but the dense accumulation of snow-cloud weakened her power to a faint twilight which was rather pervasive of the landscape than traceable to the sky. The breeze had gone down, and the rustle of their feet and tones of their speech echoed with an alert rebound from every post, boundary-stone, and ancient wall they passed, even where the distance of the echo's origin was less than a few yards. Beyond their own slight noises nothing was to be heard save the occasional bark of foxes in the direction of Yalbury Wood, or the brush of a rabbit among the grass now and then as it scampered out of their way.

Most of the outlying homesteads and hamlets had been visited by about two o'clock; they then passed across the outskirts of a wooded part toward the main village, nobody being at home at the Manor. Pursuing no recognized track, great care was necessary in walking lest their faces should come in contact with the low-hanging boughs of the old lime-trees, which in many spots formed dense overgrowths of interlaced branches . . .

By this time they were crossing to a gate in the direction of the school which, standing on a slight eminence at the junction of three ways, now rose in unvarying and dark flatness against the sky. The instruments were retuned, and all the band entered the school enclosure, enjoined by old William to keep upon the grass.

'Number seventy-eight,' he softly gave out as they formed round in a semicircle, the boys opening the lanterns to get a clearer light, and directing their rays on the books.

Then passed forth into the quiet night an ancient and time-worn hymn, embodying a quaint Christianity in words orally transmitted from father to son through several generations down to the present characters, who sang them out right earnestly:

> *Remember Adam's fall,*
> *O thou Man:*
> *Remember Adam's fall*
> *From Heaven to Hell.*
> *Remember Adam's fall;*
> *How he hath condemn'd all*
> *In Hell perpetual*
> *There for to dwell. . .*

Having concluded the last note they listened for a minute or two, but found that no sound issued from the schoolhouse.

'"Our breaths, and then, O, what unbounded goodness!", number fifty-nine,' said William.

This was duly gone through, and no notice whatever seemed to be taken of the performance.

'Good guide us, surely 'tisn't a' empty house, as befell us in the year thirty-nine and forty-three!' said old Dewy.

'Perhaps she's jist come from some musical city, and sneers at our doings?' the tranter whispered.

''Od rabbit her!' said Mr Penny, with an annihilating look at a corner of the school chimney, 'I don't quite stomach her, if this is it. Your plain music well done is as worthy as your other sort done bad, a' b'lieve, souls; so say I.'

'Four breaths, and then the last,' said the leader authoritatively. "Rejoice, ye Tenants of the Earth", number sixty-four.'

At the close, waiting yet another minute, he said in a clear loud voice, as he said in the village at that hour and season for the previous forty years –

'A merry Christmas to ye!'

* * *

Farmer Shiner's was a queer lump of a house, standing at the corner of a lane that ran into the principal thoroughfare. The upper windows were much wider than they were high, and this feature, together with a broad bay-window where the door might have been expected, gave it by day the aspect of a human countenance turned askance, and wearing a sly and wicked leer. Tonight nothing was visible but the outline of the roof upon the sky.

The front of this building was reached, and the preliminaries arranged as usual.

'Four breaths, and number thirty-two, "Behold the Morning Star"', said old William.

They had reached the end of the second verse, and the fiddlers were doing the up-bow stroke previously to pouring forth the opening chord of the third verse, when, without a light appearing or any signal being given a roaring voice exclaimed –

'Shut up, woll 'ee! Don't make your blaring row here! A feller wi' a headache enough to split his skull likes a quiet night!'

Slam went the window.

'Hullo, that's a' ugly blow for we!' said the tranter, in a keenly appreciative voice, and turning to his companions.

'Finish the carrel, all who be friends of harmony!' commanded old William; and they continued to the end.

'Four breaths, and number nineteen!' said William firmly. 'Give it him well; the quire can't be insulted in this manner!'

A light now flashed into existence, the window opened, and the farmer stood revealed as one in a terrific passion.

'Drown en! – drown en!' the tranter cried, fiddling frantically. 'Play fortissimy, and drown his spaking!'

'Fortissimy!' said Michael Mail, and the music and singing waxed so loud that it was impossible to know what Mr Shiner had said, was saying, or was about to say; but wildly flinging his arms and body about in the forms of capital Xs and Ys, he appeared to utter enough invectives to consign the whole parish to perdition.

'Very onseemly – very!' said old William, as they retired. 'Never such a dreadful scene in the whole round o' my carrel practice – never! And he a churchwarden!'

'Only a drap o' drink got into his head,' said the tranter. 'Man's well enough when he's in his religious frame. He's in his worldly frame now. Must ask en to our bit of a party to-morrow night, I suppose, and so put en in humour again. We bear no mortal man ill-will.'

THOMAS HARDY
Under the Greenwood Tree

Carollers at Mole End

It was a pretty sight, and a seasonable one, that met their eyes when they flung the door open. In the fore-court, lit by the dim rays of a horn lantern, some eight or ten little field mice stood in a semicircle, red worsted comforters round their throats, their fore-paws thrust deep into their pockets, their feet jigging for warmth. With bright beady eyes they glanced shyly at each other, sniggering a little, sniffing and applying coat-sleeves a good deal. As the door opened, one of the elder ones that carried the lantern was just, saying, 'Now then, one, two, three!' and forthwith their shrill little voices uprose on the air, singing one of the old-time carols that their forefathers composed in fields that were fallow and held by frost, or when snow-bound in chimney corners, and handed down to be sung in the miry street to lamp-lit windows at Yuletime.

CAROL

Villagers all, this frosty tide,
Let your doors swing open wide,
Though wind may follow, and snow beside,
Yet draw us in by your fire to bide;
  Joy shall be yours in the morning!

Here we stand in the cold and the sleet,
Blowing fingers and stamping feet,
Come from far away you to greet –
You by the fire and we in the street –
  Bidding you joy in the morning!

For ere one half of the night was gone,
Sudden a star has led us on,
Raining bliss and benison –
Bliss to-morrow and more anon,
  Joy for every morning!

Goodman Joseph toiled through the snow –
Saw the star o'er a stable low;
Mary she might not further go –
Welcome thatch, and litter below!
    Joy was hers in the morning!

And then they heard the angels tell
'Who were the first to cry Nowell?
Animals all, as it befell,
In the stable where they did dwell!
    Joy shall be theirs in the morning!'

The voices ceased, the singers, bashful but smiling, exchanged sidelong glances, and silence succeeded – but for a moment only. Then, from up above and far away, down the tunnel they had so lately travelled was borne to their ears in a faint musical hum the sound of distant bells ringing a joyous and dangerous peal.

'Very well sung, boys!' cried the Rat heartily. 'And now come along in, all of you, and warm yourselves by the fire, and have something hot!'

KENNETH GRAHAME
The Wind in the Willows

The Oxen

Christmas Eve, and twelve of the clock,
   'Now they are all on their knees',
An elder said as we sat in a flock
   By the embers in hearthside ease.

We pictured the meek mild creatures where
   They dwelt in their strawy pen,
Nor did it occur to one of us there
   To doubt they were kneeling then.

So fair a fancy few would weave
   In these years! Yet, I feel,
If some one said on Christmas Eve,
   'Come; see the oxen kneel

'In the lonely barton by yonder coomb
   Our childhood used to know',
I should go with him in the gloom,
   Hoping it might be so.

THOMAS HARDY

Noel: Christmas Eve, 1913
Pax hominibus bonae voluntatis

A frosty Christmas Eve
   When the stars were shining
Fared I forth alone
   where westwards falls this hill,
And from many a village
   in the water's valley
Distant music reach'd me
   peals of bells aringing;
The constellated sounds
   ran sprinkling on earth's floor
As the dark vault above
   with stars spangled o'er.
Then sped my thought to keep
   that first Christmas of all
When the shepherds watching
   by their folds ere the dawn
Heard music in the fields
   and marvelling could not tell
Whether it were angels
   or the bright stars singing.
Now blessed be the tow'rs
   that crown England so fair
That stand up strong in prayer
   unto God for our souls:
Blessed be their founders
   (said I) an' our country folk
Who are ringing for Christ
   in the belfries tonight
With arms lifted to clutch
   the rattling ropes that race
Into the dark above
   and the mad romping din.

But to me afar
   it was starry music
Angel's song, comforting
   as the comfort of Christ
When he spake tenderly
   to his sorrowful flock:
The old words came to me
   by the riches of time
Mellow'd and transfigured
   as I stood on the hill
Heark'ning in the aspect
   of th'eternal silence.

ROBERT BRIDGES

Moonless darkness stands between

Moonless darkness stands between.
Past, O Past, no more be seen!
But the Bethlehem star may lead me
To the sight of Him who freed me
From the self that I have been.
Make me pure, Lord: Thou art holy:
Make me meek, Lord: Thou wert lowly;
Now beginning, and alway:
Now begin, on Christmas day.

GERARD MANLEY HOPKINS

Welcome!

Welcome, all wonders in one sight!
  Eternity shut in a span!
Summer in winter! day in night!
  Heaven in earth! and God in man!
Great little One, whose all-embracing birth,
  Lifts earth to heaven, stoops heaven to earth.

RICHARD CRASHAW

'I heard him. He said Bethlehem.'

The service went on, a monotonous sleepy noise to which Audrey paid very little attention . . . quite a lot of feathers came out of Mrs Oliphant's cushion every time she sat down. She had a special small red cushion to herself, in case the pew gave her lumbago. It got thinner every Sunday because no one ever mended the hole in the corner.

Behind the chrysanthemums and holly the choirboys were sucking cough-drops and whispering whilst Mr Bunny read the lessons. A man in the back row leaned over and hit one of them a loud 'blip' on the head with a Prayer Book. Neither the boy nor Mr Bunny took any notice, and Miss Constance at the organ was quietly setting up the music, but Audrey saw the man looking ruefully at the cover of the book.

Mr Bunny read the lessons in a big, booming voice which hit a pillar and came back, like a second person muttering the lesson after him. His mouth made a hole in his white beard. He had a trick of working his hands up inside the arms of his surplice as he read. Audrey watched him. Suppose he got them stuck up there? Would anyone be allowed to help him get them out, or would the service have to stop?

All at once she sat up, straight and stiff, listening.

Mr Bunny had said 'Bethlehem'.

Mother had said that, and Ellen . . . she pulled at Catherine's skirt, but Catherine's face had a far-off look. Perhaps she was going over her week's accounts in her head, like Mrs Power.

Bethlehem. Then that was a true story. Not a home story. . . Then the little baby who came from a heaven of gold to lie in a cold stable . . . the baby for whom the bells were rung last night . . . then that baby, and Bethlehem, had something to do with church, and Mr Bunny.

Audrey sat, disturbed and critical. Long afterwards, when the fairy baby had become a human child in a great human story, she was still perplexed and critical. For the child who was born in a stable, preached by the wayside, and died upon a hill, seemed, as she grew older, to have less and less to do with the inside of a church.

Outside the church, Audrey danced on the frosty stones, running round and round Catherine, eager for an explanation.

'Mother. Mr Bunny said Bethlehem. I heard him. He said Bethlehem.'

'Audrey! You mustn't call Mr Brere, Mr Bunny.'

'Daddy does.'

The light of argument lit in Audrey's eyes. She forgot Bethlehem.

ELIZABETH CAMBRIDGE
Hostages to Fortune

The Heavenly Light

The Incarnation did not alter anything, it only revealed the love of God. One night, so to speak, a heavenly light was switched on to earth and men *saw* a baby Face, and *that* was God.

FATHER ANDREW
The Melody of Life

Chanticleer's Carol

All this night shrill chanticleer,
Day's proclaiming trumpeter,
  Claps his wings and loudly cries,
  Mortals, mortals, wake and rise!
    See a wonder
    Heaven is under;
  From the earth is risen a Sun
  Shines all night, though day be done.

Wake, O earth, wake everything!
Wake and hear the joy I bring;
  Wake and joy; for all this night
  Heaven and every twinkling light,
    All amazing
    Still stand gazing.
  Angels, Powers, and all that be,
  Wake, and joy this Sun to see.

Hail, O Sun, O blessed Light,
Sent into the world by night!
  Let thy rays and heavenly powers
  Shine in these dark souls of ours;
    For most duly
    Thou art truly
  God and man, we do confess:
  Hail, O Sun of Righteousness!

WILLIAM AUSTIN

New Prince, New Pomp

Behold a silly tender babe
 In freezing winter nigh
In homely manger trembling lies:
 Alas! a piteous sight.

The inns are full; no man will yield
 This little pilgrim bed;
But forced he is with silly beasts
 In crib to shroud his head.

Despise not him for lying there;
 First what he is inquire:
An orient pearl is often found
 In depth of dirty mire.

Weigh not his crib, his wooden dish,
 Nor beasts that by him feed;
Weigh not his mother's poor attire,
 Nor Joseph's simple weed.

This stable is a Prince's court,
 This crib his chair of state,
The beasts are parcel of his pomp,
 The wooden dish his plate.

The persons in that poor attire
 His royal liveries wear;
The Prince himself is come from heaven.
 This pomp is prizèd there.

With joy approach, O Christian wight,
 Do homage to thy King;
And highly praise this humble pomp
 Which he from heaven doth bring.

ROBERT SOUTHWELL

Et Incarnatus Est

Love is the plant of peace and most precious of virtues;
For heaven hold it ne might so heavy it seemed,
Till it had on earth yoten himself.
Was never leaf upon linden lighter thereafter,
As when it had of the fold flesh and blood taken;
Then was it portative and piercing as the point of a needle.
May no armour it let, neither high walls.
For-thy is love leader of our Lord's folk of heaven.

WILLIAM LANGLAND

---

yoten: poured out; *fold*: earth; *For-thy*: therefore

Christmas with an imprisoned people

I climbed down the narrow steps under the Church of the Nativity in Bethlehem on Christmas Eve, and knelt by the silver star that marks the traditional site of the manger. Bishop Riah had just led the annual carol service in one of the chapels. It was well attended by visitors, but few local Anglicans were present.

There were no Christmas decorations in the streets of Bethlehem this year. Although the Israelis, desperate to attract foreign tourists, said that they would relax the checkpoints this Christmas, most Palestinians remained prisoners in their own country.

I had gone with Bishop Riah and the other Heads of Churches to Ramallah, to visit the leaders of the Palestinian Authority. It was the final day of mourning for Yasser Arafat, and the day before Tony Blair's brief visit. For many Palestinians, Mr Blair is just a war criminal; but there is a slim hope that he might be able to influence President Bush to move away from blanket support for Israel.

We began our Christmas Eve celebrations in Shepherds' Fields, singing carols in the cave where people may first have heard of the baby's birth. Walking in their steps down to the town, a Palestinian woman spoke of how the new wall was disrupting her life: 'They want to block out the sun,' she told me, 'but we will always look up and hope to see the star.'

MICHAEL DOE

Prayer

Lord, I will go to Mary and make covenant with her, to keep her child, not for her need but for mine. And take to me the sweet child and swathe Him in his cradle with love bands. Lord, help me to put from me the cradle of self love and draw to me the cradle of true love, for that liketh this child to rest Him in, and so in my soul sing lovelike and say:

> *Lovely little child, fairest of hue,*
> *Have mercy on me, sweet Jesu.*

And while I thus sing I will be sorry and think how oft I have received my God and laid Him in a foul common stable to all the seven deadly sins . . . and seldom fully cleansed to God's liking; therefore oft sigh and sorrow and shrive me to God as I rock the cradle, and sing and say: Lovely little Child.

ANONYMOUS

Balulalow

O my dear heart, young Jesus sweet,
Prepare thy cradle in my spreit,
And I sail rock thee in my heart,
And never mair from thee depart.

But I sail praise thee evermore,
With sangis sweet unto thy gloir;
The knees of my heart shall I bow,
And sing that richt *Balulalow*.

THE BROTHERS WEDDERBURN

spreit: spirit; *sall*: shall; *sangis*: songs; *gloir*: glory

I only knew he named my name

This excerpt from a very long poem gives the resolution to Browning's struggle between faith in its traditional form and intellectual and religious integrity – a struggle which increases in intensity for us. He is 'woolgathering' during a foolish sermon in an unaccustomed chapel on Christmas Eve . . .

. . . While I watched my foolish heart expand
In the lazy glow of benevolence,
   O'er the various modes of man's belief.
I sprang up with fear's vehemence.
   Needs must there be one way, our chief
Best way of worship: let me strive
To find it, and when found, contrive
My fellows also take their share!
This constitutes my earthly care:
God's is above and distinct.
For I, a man, with men am linked
And not a brute with brutes; no gain
That I experience, must remain
Unshared: but should my best endeavour
To share it, fail – subsisteth ever
God's care above, and I exult
That God, by God's own ways occult,
May – doth, I will believe – bring back
All wanderers to a single track.
Meantime, I can but testify
God's care for me – no more, can I –
It is but for myself I know;
   The world rolls witnessing around me
   Only to leave me as it found me;
Men cry there, but my ear is slow;
Their races flourish or decay
– What boots it, while yon lucid way

Loaded with stars divides the vault?
But soon my soul repairs its fault
When, sharpening sense's hebetude,
She turns on my own life! So viewed,
No mere mote's-breadth but teems immense
With witnessings of providence:
And woe to me if when I look
Upon that record, the sole book
Unsealed to me, I take no heed
Of any warning that I read!
Have I been sure, this Christmas-Eve,
God's own hand did the rainbow weave,
Whereby the truth from heaven slid
Into my soul? – I cannot bid
The world admit he stooped to heal
My soul, as if in a thunder-peal
Where one heard noise, and one saw flame,
I only knew he named my name . . .

ROBERT BROWNING
Christmas Eve and Easter Day

Christmas Present

I make no apology for including this snatch of A Christmas Carol. For its sheer exuberance there is nothing to beat it – a model for all our New Year's resolutions. Scrooge wakes on Christmas morning from a vision of his loveless life and his future unmourned death.

Yes! and the bedpost was his own. The bed was his own, the room was his own. Best and happiest of all, the Time before him was his own, to make amends in!

'I will live in the Past, the Present, and the Future!' Scrooge repeated, as he scrambled out of bed. 'The Spirits of all Three shall strive within me. Oh Jacob Marley! Heaven, and the Christmas Time be praised for this! I say it on my knees, old Jacob, on my knees!'

He was so fluttered and so glowing with his good intentions, that his broken voice would scarcely answer to his call. He had been sobbing violently in his conflict with the Spirit, and his face was wet with tears.

'They are not torn down,' cried Scrooge, folding one of his bed-curtains in his arms, 'they are not torn down, rings and all. They are here: I am here: the shadows of the things that would have been may be dispelled. They will be, I know they will!'

His hands were busy with his garments all this time: turning them inside out, putting them on upside down, tearing them, mislaying them, making them parties to every kind of extravagance.

'I don't know what to do!' cried Scrooge, laughing and crying in the same breath; and making a perfect Laocoön of himself with his stockings. 'I am as light as a feather, I am as happy as an angel, I am as merry as a schoolboy. I am as giddy as a drunken man. A Merry Christmas to everybody! A Happy New Year to all the world. Hallo there! Whoop! Hallo!'

He had frisked into the sitting-room, and was now standing there: perfectly winded.

'There's the saucepan that the gruel was in!' cried Scrooge, starting off again, and frisking round the fireplace. 'There's the door, by which the Ghost of Jacob Marley entered! There's the corner where the Ghost of Christmas Present sat! There's the window where I saw the wandering Spirits! It's all right, it's all true, it all happened. Ha, ha, ha!'

Really, for a man who had been out of practice for so many years, it was a splendid laugh, a most illustrious laugh. The father of a long, long line of brilliant laughs!

'I don't know what day of the month it is!' said Scrooge. 'I don't know how long I've been among the Spirits. I don't know anything. I'm quite a baby. Never mind. I don't care. I'd rather be a baby. Hallo! Whoop! Hallo there!' He was checked in his transports by the churches ringing out the lustiest peals he had ever heard. Clash, clang, hammer, ding, dong, bell. Bell, dong, ding, hammer, clang, clash! Oh, glorious, glorious!

Running to the window, he opened it, and put out his head. No fog, no mist; clear, bright, jovial, stirring, cold; cold, piping for the blood to dance to; golden sunlight; heavenly sky; sweet fresh air; merry bells. Oh glorious. Glorious!

'What's today?' cried Scrooge, calling downward to a boy in Sunday clothes, who perhaps had loitered in to look about him.

'EH?' returned the boy, with all his might of wonder.

'What's today, my fine fellow?' said Scrooge.

'Today!' replied the boy. 'Why, CHRISTMAS DAY.'

* * *

He dressed himself 'all in his best', and at last got out into the streets. The people were by this time pouring forth, as he had seen them with the Ghost of Christmas Present; and walking with his hands behind him, Scrooge regarded everyone with a delighted smile. He looked so irresistibly pleasant, in a word, that three or four good-humoured fellows said, 'Good morning, Sir! A Merry Christmas to you!' And Scrooge said often afterwards, that of all the blithe sounds he had ever heard, those were the blithest in his ears.

He had not gone far, when coming on towards him he beheld the portly gentleman, who had walked into his counting-house the day before and said, 'Scrooge and Marley's, I believe?'. It sent a pang across his heart to think how this old gentleman would look upon him when they met; but he knew what path lay straight before him, and he took it.

'My dear Sir,' said Scrooge, quickening his pace, and taking the old gentleman by both his hands. 'How do you do? I hope you succeeded yesterday. It was very kind of you. A Merry Christmas to you, Sir!'

'Mr. Scrooge?'

'Yes,' said Scrooge. 'That is my name, and I fear it may not be pleasant to you. Allow me to ask your pardon. And will you have the goodness' – here Scrooge whispered in his ear.

'Lord bless me!' cried the gentleman, as if his breath were gone. 'My dear Mr. Scrooge, are you serious?'

'If you please,' said Scrooge. 'Not a farthing less. A great many back-payments are included in it, I assure you. Will you do me that favour?'

'My dear Sir,' said the other, shaking hands with him. 'I don't know what to say to such munifi-'

'Don't say anything, please,' retorted Scrooge. 'Come and see me. Will you come and see me?'

'I will!' cried the old gentleman. And it was clear he meant to do it.

'Thank'ee,' said Scrooge. 'I am much obliged to you. I thank you fifty times. Bless you!'

He went to church, and walked about the streets, and watched the people hurrying to and fro, and patted children on the head, and questioned beggars, and looked down into the kitchens of houses, and up to the windows; and found that everything could yield him pleasure. He had never dreamed that any walk – that anything – could give him so much happiness.

CHARLES DICKENS
A Christmas Carol

No Small Wonder

Small wonder the kings,
small wonder they bore
the gold and the incense,
the myrrh to adore;
but God gives his life on a cross -
no small wonder!

Small wonder the love,
small wonder the grace,
the power, the glory,
the light of his face;
but all to redeem my poor heart -
no small wonder!

Small wonder the star,
small wonder the light,
the angels in chorus,
the shepherds in fright;
but stable and manger for God -
no small wonder!

http://paulwigmore.co.uk
Jubilate hymns

One of the most frequently sung Christmas carols is 'No Small Wonder' and it actually began because of a mental tic.

In November 1983 I had that annoying experience, suffered by most people now and then, a short, everyday phrase repeating itself in my head over and over again. The phrase was simply, 'small wonder'. Someone must have said it within my hearing. I longed to be rid of it. I wondered if just writing it down over and over again several times would do it. So I tried it. The sheet of repeated words made me aware of its simple waltz-like rhythm.

(Try saying 'small wonder, small wonder, small wonder' aloud, keeping a steady, regular beat.)

And in the hazy, stumbling process that is fancifully called 'inspiration', a poem emerged.

On November 18 and fairly pleased with the result I sent it to the composer and a good friend Paul Edwards. He wrote shortly afterwards, enclosing his setting. He said my letter and poem had arrived just as he was about to take his laundry to the local launderette, so he had taken it with him, plus some manuscript paper. After putting his clothes into the machine he had sat down opposite it, watching the contents going round and round as he worked on a tune. And that lovely tune emerged, shining.

'No Small Wonder' seems to have been well-liked from the time it was published; it became the publisher's best-seller; the Choir of King's College, Cambridge performed it for BBC Television at Christmas 2000 and my Performing Rights Society records show that it is being recorded and broadcast from cathedrals and churches round the world every Christmas.

Then, in 2008, I had the excitement of discovering that the BBC Music Magazine had conducted a poll among cathedral choir directors, organists or composers, asking each of them to name five of their favourite Christmas carols, ancient or modern. Out of the 50 carols chosen, both well-established and modern, 'No Small Wonder' was 19th.

One evening [some years earlier] while I was reading to [Sir John] Betjeman from one of his favourite writers, Harry Williams, he interrupted me as I read, and said, 'You know, I can see you're a poet.'

Now, that sort of thing does wonders for a man, and especially for introverted, inveterate braggers like me.

PAUL WIGMORE

What sweeter music can we bring?

What sweeter music can we bring
Than a carol, for to sing
The birth of this our heavenly King?
Awake the voice! Awake the string:

We see him come, and know him ours,
Who with his sunshine and his showers
Turns all the patient ground to flowers.

Dark and dull night, fly hence away,
And give the honour to this day,
That sees December turned to May,
If we may ask the reason, say:

The darling of the world is come,
And fit it is we find a room
To welcome him. The nobler part
Of all the house here is the heart:

Which we will give him, and bequeath
This holly and this ivy wreath,
To do him honour who's our King,
And Lord of all this revelling:

ROBERT HERRICK

Christmas Expectations

Gradually there gathered the feeling of expectation. Christmas was coming. In the shed, at nights, a secret candle was burning, a sound of veiled voices was heard. The boys were learning the old mystery play of St George and Beelzebub. Twice a week, by lamplight, there was choir practice in the church, for the learning of old carols Brangwen wanted to hear. The girls went to these practices. Everywhere was a sense of mystery and rousedness. Everybody was preparing for something.

The time came near, the girls were decorating the church, with cold fingers binding holly and fir and yew about the pillars, till a new spirit was in the church, the stone broke out into dark, rich leaf, the arches put forth their buds, and cold flowers rose to blossom in the dim, mystic atmosphere. Ursula must weave mistletoe over the door, and over the screen, and hang a silver dove from a sprig of yew, till dusk came down, and the church was a grove.

In the cow-shed the boys were blacking their faces for a dress rehearsal; the turkey hung dead, with opened, speckled wings, in the dairy. The time was come to make pies, in readiness.

The expectation grew more tense. The star was risen into the sky, the songs, the carols were ready to hail it. The star was the sign in the sky. Earth too should give a sign. As evening drew on, hearts beat fast with anticipation, hands were full of ready gifts. There were the tremulously expectant words of the church service, the night was past and the morning was come, the gifts were given and received, joy and peace made a flapping of wings in each heart, there was a great burst of carols, the Peace of the World had dawned, strife had passed away, every hand was linked in hand, every heart was singing.

It was bitter, though, that Christmas day, as it drew on to evening and night, became a sort of bank holiday, flat and stale. The morning was so wonderful, but in the afternoon and the evening the ecstasy perished like a nipped thing, like a bud in false spring. Alas, that Christmas was only a domestic feast, a feast of sweetmeats and toys! Why did not the grown-ups also change their everyday hearts, and give way to ecstasy? Where was the ecstasy?

D H LAWRENCE
The Rainbow

☆

Keeping Christmas

Keeping Christmas

It is now Christmas, and not a Cup of drinke must passe without a Caroll, the Beasts, Fowle and Fish, come to generall execution, and the Corn is ground to dust for the Bakehouse, and the Pastry: Cards and Dice purge many a purse . . . now good cheere and welcome, and God be with you, and I thanke you: and against the new yeere, provide for the presents: the Lord of Misrule is no meane man for his time, and the ghests of the high Table must lacke no Wine: the lusty bloods must looke about them like men, and piping the dauncing puts away much melancholy: ... a good fire heats all the house, and a full Almes-basket makes the Beggars Prayers: . . . Swearers and Swaggerers are sent away to the Alehouse, and unruly Wenches goe in danger of Judgement: Musicians now make their Instruments speake out, and a good song is worth the hearing. In summe, it is holy time, a duty in Christians, for the remembrance of Christ, and custome among friends, for the maintenance of good fellowship: in briefe, I thus conclude of it: I hold it a memory of the Heavens Love, and the worlds peace, the myrth of the honest, and the meeting of the friendly.

NICHOLAS BRETON

Keeping Christmas at Fairacres

At Christmas, as at every season, our worship is closely interwoven with the rest of our life: smells of roasting turkey waft from kitchen to chapel; sisters come with hands stained from preparing Brussels sprouts to feed 40; with veil awry after a morning with the polisher; with a mind still rephrasing a difficult letter, or with a heart delighted by a kindness received. A hymn, a psalm or two, a verse of scripture and a prayer, is sometimes enough to remind us that our praise and that of the angels is a single song. If not for me, perhaps it is for the sister opposite; if not today, then tomorrow, God willing.

Christmas Day begins later than usual: matins is at 6.30 a.m., and is followed by breakfast with home-made rolls, lemon curd or honey, coffee and fruit. It's a silent meal, and is followed by an hour or so of personal prayer. The office of terce is the transition to necessary work: we have brought to a fine art getting a Christmas lunch ready by 11.30 (turkey, sprouts, carrots, roast potatoes, gravy and stuffing, mince pies and the rest), so that we can all go to another eucharist (because the middle of the day is the time when almost every sister is able to come, and because there is more to hear and sing and give thanks for).

Lunch follows, shared with friends as well as those who are staying with us. Sometimes a sister or group will have worked on a centrepiece for each table, or decorations for the windows. The refectory has its own tree and crib, and there are many candles. Everyone helps to clear and wash up before none, and there is free time for a walk or a snooze, conversation by the fire, or the Queen's Speech on television.

Tea is available for those who can find room for it, and later in the afternoon the community gathers to share news and to unwrap some of the presents we've been given. People are touchingly generous to us, and opening gifts takes place over several days.

Before vespers, our guests join us for a candlelit procession into chapel, where we have a time of informal intercessions and carols around the crib. By naming the people and places and situations in our own hearts, we try to put into words the prayer that is the undercurrent of all our celebration. We sing it at the end of vespers on Christmas Eve in Laurence Housman's words:

> O perfect Love, outpassing sight,
> O light beyond our ken,
> Come down through all the world tonight
> And heal the hearts of men.

The day ends with compline, sending us to our beds with the familiar words of confession and forgiveness, and of God's blessing us with peace.

SR CATHERINE AND SR CLARE-LOUISE SLG

A Christmas Family Party

A Christmas family-party! We know nothing in nature more delightful! There seems a magic in the very name of Christmas. Petty jealousies and discords are forgotten: social feelings are awakened in bosoms to which they have long been strangers: father and son, or brother and sister, who have met and passed with averted gaze, or a look of cold recognition, for months before, proffer and return the cordial embrace, and bury their past animosities in their present happiness. Kindly hearts that have yearned towards each other, but have been withheld by false notions of pride and self-dignity, are again reunited, and all is kindness and benevolence! Would that Christmas lasted the whole year through, and that the prejudices and passions which deform our better nature, were never called into action among those to whom they should ever be strangers!

The Christmas family-party that we mean, is not a mere assemblage of relations, got up at a week or two's notice, originating this year, having no family precedent in the last, and not likely to be repeated in the next. It is an annual gathering of all the accessible members of the family, young or old, rich or poor; and all the children look forward to it, for two months beforehand, in a fever of anticipation . . .

CHARLES DICKENS
Sketches by Boz

This new and shining thing

Audrey stood and looked at the Christmas tree. She had had a good tea, though not as good as she would have liked, or could have managed. Now there was this new and shining thing. The little spindling thuya which she had seen, dusty and lonely, in its pot, stood translated. Its spiky boughs stood out stiffly, bright with red, yellow, and pink butterflies, hot and shimmering with candles.

The points of the flames strained upwards, there was a smell of warm wax. She was too happy to shout or sing. She was so happy that she had a hollow feeling in the pit of her stomach. It hurt, yet she wished that this minute could go on for ever. The wonderful tree was true. It was much truer than walks, and tooth-brushing and being put to bed, and all the things that happened every day... Someone threw on a log and with a crash the fire reddened and a shower of sparks flew up, like goldfinches disturbed in wayside thistles.

Catherine pushed parcels into her hand to give round. Audrey stood glumly, looking down at them. She wanted to go on looking at the tree. Ungraciously, quickly, she pushed them into the hands of the family, sitting round on chairs. Then she stood looking... Two things to watch at once ... the opening of the parcel and the surprised and pleased face of the person who was opening it.

Catherine rolled up string and folded brown paper, rescued useful cardboard boxes and labels. Audrey and Adam were hurrying through their own parcels now, quickly, skimpily, with one eye on the tree.

It was going well. It was going to be all right. They all looked comfortable, settled. The critical chill of the beginning had thawed out. The candles had long black wicks, and there was a smell of hot pine needles. Spatters of wax were falling on the floor, flames shot and towered. William began to blow candles out, puffing his cheeks and making a great fuss. Everyone laughed. Audrey ran round the tree crying out: 'Look! Come! Here's another!'

Somebody was blowing up a balloon. Adam was winding up a mechanical engine and letting it run down again, wheels in air. Everyone was eating chocolates.

Catherine gave Adam his toy horse and Audrey her doll, Adam patted the horse all over, slowly, his face grave and puzzled. Almost he seemed afraid of it. Audrey turned her doll up and looked at its cotton drawers, pulled its frock down over its fat pink stockinette thighs, prodded its eyes, and dropped it face downwards on the floor. A thin wailing pierced the noise in the room.

I saw three ships coom sai-iling in.

William hunted in his pockets.

'Poor little devils! Fancy having nothing better than that to do on Christmas night!' The voices swelled as Irene opened the front door.

And 'oo d'you think was in them then,

in them then, in them then, Joseph and hi'is young lydy!

'Sheer blasphemy,' Mrs Gregory said, nearly choking over chocolate. 'Don't give them a penny. Not one penny.'

William dumped the coppers into Audrey's hands.

'Run out, kiddy. That'll stop 'em.'

Catherine took the hall lamp and went out with Audrey. A row of children's faces swam up suddenly out of the darkness outside.

Now Christmas is 'ere, they chanted:

We wish you good che-er, We wish you a merry Christmas and a Happy New Year.

Round eyes, blinking in the lamplight, round red noses, open mouths, bright-coloured mufflers crossed on their chests. They looked like young birds waiting to be fed. Audrey dumped all the coppers into the nearest hand.

'Now then ... g'way!' she said firmly.

She didn't want them to go. She thought 'Three Ships' was beautiful. Even better than 'Abey my Boy' or 'Who's your lady friend?' and the other things that those lucky creatures, the children who were allowed out after dark, sang in the streets.

The children grabbed the money and ran, their boots clattering up the frosty street.

'Poor little beggars,' said Catherine.

'Young varmints,' said Irene, slamming the door. 'I'd learn them to beg. My mother she warmed our Maggie to rights, the only time she went out carolling.'

Adam had got Audrey's doll. He was hugging it, mutely but protectively. The creature's pink arm hung down over his wrist, he stroked its head, crooning softly. Catherine drew an unhappy breath, awaiting outcry and violence from Audrey.

Audrey walked straight across the room to the wooden horse and ran round with it, banging the wheels and shouting. Her curls bobbed, her eyes were bright. Catherine looked at the pair of them. Well! You never knew!

She sat down on the floor at William's feet and rested her head against him. Two balloons were being tossed about. Gregory's wife and Edward's wife were talking frocks, nobody noticed the noise that Audrey was making.

William put his hand on her shoulder. He was glad that his family had chosen his house to meet in. It wasn't really central, but they had all come. He was proud of Catherine and of Audrey and Adam, and of the pair of home-grown cockerels they'd had for lunch. He'd never bought a pair of birds like that anywhere else, so large and yet so tender. That was a good cake Catherine had made, too. Dark and close, and full of bits of peel. This sort of thing was what he worked for, wasn't it?

He liked the black ribbon in Catherine's hair. She was a nice-looking wench, when she wasn't overtired or untidy. A messy worker... but a trier. He pressed his hand a little harder on her shoulder, and wished that life allowed them more of such evenings.

ELIZABETH CAMBRIDGE
Hostages to Fortune

Family Reunions

The discordance or discomfort complained of by modern critics, in the family reunion, is not due to that mystical focal fire having been left burning, but to its having been left to go cold. It is because cold fragments of a once living thing are clumsily lumped together; it is no argument against making the thing alive. Christmas toys are incongruously dangled before heavy and heathen uncles who wish they were playing golf. But that does not alter the fact that they might become much brighter and more intelligent if they knew how to play with toys; and they are horrible bores about golf. Their dullness is only the last deadly product of the mechanical progress of organized and professional sports, in that rigid world of routine outside the home. When they were children, behind closed doors in the home, it is probable that nearly every one of them had daydreams and unwritten dramas that belonged to them as much as Hamlet belonged to Shakespeare or Pickwick to Dickens. How much more thrilling it would be if Uncle Henry, instead of describing in detail all the strokes with which he ought to have got out of the bunker, were to say frankly that he had been on a voyage to the end of the world and had just caught the Great Sea-Serpent. How much more truly intellectual would be the conversation of Uncle William if, instead of telling us the point to which he had reduced his handicap, he could still say with conviction that he was King of the Kangaroo Islands, or Chief of the Rango Dango Redskins . . .

G K CHESTERTON
The Thing

The Pooters' Christmas

December 19. The annual invitation came to spend Christmas with Carrie's mother – the usual family festive gathering, to which we always look forward. Lupin declined to go. I was astounded and expressed my surprise and disgust. Lupin then obliged us with the following Radical speech: 'I hate a family gathering at Christmas. What does it mean? Why someone says: "Ah! we miss poor Uncle James, who was here last year," and we all begin to snivel. Someone else says: "It's two years since poor Aunt Liz used to sit in that corner". Then we all begin to snivel again. Then another gloomy relation says: "Ah! I wonder whose turn it will be next?" Then we all snivel again, and proceed to eat and drink too much; and they don't discover until I get up that we have been seated thirteen at dinner.'

Lupin spends Christmas with the family of his fiancée.

Christmas Day. We caught the 10.20 train at Paddington, and spent a pleasant day at Carrie's mother's. The country was quite nice and pleasant, although the roads were sloppy. We dined in the middle of the day, just ten of us, and talked over old times. If everybody had a nice, uninterfering mother-in-law, such as I have, what a deal of happiness there would be in the world. Being all in good spirits, I proposed her health; and I made, I think, a very good speech.

I concluded, rather neatly, by saying: 'On an occasion like this – whether relatives, friends or acquaintances – we are all inspired with good feelings towards each other. We are of one mind, and think only of love and friendship. Those who have quarrelled with absent friends should kiss and make it up. Those who happily have *not* fallen out, can kiss all the same.'

I saw the tears in the eyes of both Carrie and her mother, and must say I felt very flattered by the compliment. That dear old Reverend John Panzy Smith, who married us, made a most cheerful and amusing speech, and said he should act on my suggestion respecting the kissing. He then walked round the table and kissed all the ladies, including Carrie. Of course one did not object to this; but I was more than staggered when a young fellow named Moss, who was a stranger to me, and who had scarcely spoken a word through dinner, jumped up suddenly with a sprig of mistletoe, and exclaimed: 'Hulloh! I don't see why I shouldn't be in on this scene.' Before one could realize what he was about to do, he kissed Carrie and the rest of the ladies.

Fortunately the matter was treated as a joke, and we all laughed; but it was a dangerous experiment, and I felt very uneasy for a moment as to the result...

GEORGE AND WEEDON GROSSMITH
The Diary of a Nobody

A Quaker's Christmas, 1841

Christmas eve festivities. We were amongst a select few invited
by Sterling's little people to witness the unfolding of a mighty-
mystery which has occupied their small brains for the last week.
The folding doors of the drawing-room being thrown open, the
inner room appeared like a blaze of light & luxury. In the centre
stood a fir tree reaching nearly to the ceiling, covered in all
direction with lighted tapers & various gay & glittering symbols,
while pendant from the lower branches were numerous presents
for children and guests. Papa's ingenious irony had placed a
foolscap on the top, immediately overshadowing the man in the
moon & the Pope of Rome; crowns & helmets, paper flags &
necklaces sparkled amongst the foliage & we all, old children and
young, gave ourselves up to the enthusiasm of the moment. My
present was a beautiful ivory pen tipped with silver & wreathed
with laurel, a most elegant compliment. A.M. & C. were given
some very fine engravings. The excitement having somewhat
subsided I put off a volcano in the garden. The abandon of the
children to their supreme delight was beautiful.

BARCLAY FOX

A Victorian Christmas in Herefordshire
Tuesday, 24 December, Christmas Eve

Very hard frost. Brilliant sunshine on sparkling snow. After breakfast I went to the Old Weston to see the poor Davieses and comfort them concerning their child. On the road I met David Davies the father, the shepherd at the Weston, on his way to the village to order the coffin and to the Churchyard to mark out the ground for the grave. He told me it was not Andrew as I had been informed and supposed, but little Davie who was dead. The father seemed greatly distressed and indignant because he thought the child's life had been thrown away by some mistake of the doctor. I went on to the house of mourning. Margaret Davies seemed very glad to see me and her humble gratitude for my visit was most touching. She took me upstairs into the room where the dead child was lying on the bed and turned down the sheet from his face. I never saw death look so beautiful. There was no bandage round the chin. The pretty innocent child face looked as peaceful and natural as if the child were asleep and the dark curls lay upon the little pillow. I could hardly believe he was dead. Leaving the face still uncovered the poor mother knelt with me by the little bedside while I prayed for them all. She was deeply touched and most humbly grateful. Before I left the room I stooped and kissed the child's forehead, and the mother did the same. It was as cold and as hard as marble. This is always a fresh surprise. I had not touched death for more than 30 years, and it brought back the sudden shock that I felt when as a child I was taken into a room at Hardenhuish Rectory where our little sister lay dead and was told to touch her hand.

Margaret Davies told me that before little Davie died he saw a number of people and some pretty children dancing in a beautiful garden and heard some sweet music. Then someone seems to have called him for he answered, 'What do you want with me?' He also saw beautiful birds, and the men of Weston (who carried him to his funeral). He thought his little sister Margaret was throwing ice and snow on him. (The snow fell on the coffin at the burial.) On the road I overtook Miss Stokes and went into the Old Court with her but before Kate could come and speak to me my nose began to bleed and I was obliged to fly.

Wednesday, Christmas Day

Very hard frost last night. At Presteign the thermometer fell to 2 degrees, showing 30 degrees of frost. At Monnington it fell to 4. Last night is said to have been the coldest night for 100 years. The windows of the house and Church were so thick with frost rime that we could not see out. We could not look through the Church windows all day. Snow lay on the ground and the day was dark and gloomy with a murky sky. A fair morning congregation considering the weather. By Miss Newton's special desire Dora and I went to the Cottage to eat our Christmas dinner at 1.30 immediately after service.

Immediately after dinner I had to go back to the church for the funeral of little Davie of the Old Weston who died on Monday was fixed for 2.15. The weather was dreadful, the snow driving in blinding clouds and the walking tiresome. Yet the funeral was only 20 minutes late. The Welcome Home, as it chimed softly and slowly to greet the little pilgrim coming to his rest, sounded bleared and muffled through the thick snowy air. The snow fell thickly all through the funeral service and at the service by the grave a kind woman offered her umbrella which a kind young fellow came and held over my head. The woman and man were Mrs Richards and William Jackson. I asked the poor mourners to come in and rest and warm themselves but they would not and went into Church. The poor father, David Davies the shepherd, was crying bitterly for the loss of his little lamb. Owing to the funeral it was rather late before we began the afternoon service. There were very few people in Church beside the mourners. The afternoon was very dark. I was obliged to move close to the great south window to read the Lessons and could hardly see even then. I preached from Luke ii.7. 'There was no room for them in the inn,5 and connected the little bed in the churchyard in which we had laid Davie to rest with the manger cradle at Bethlehem.

In spite of the heavy and deep snow there was a fair congregation at Brobury Church. I walked there with Powell. The water was out in Brobury lane. As we came back a thaw had set in and rain fell. By Miss Newton's special wish I went to the Cottage and spent the evening with Dora. The Cottage servants had invited the Vicarage servants to tea and supper and they came into the drawing room after supper and sang some Christmas Carols.

FRANCIS KILVERT

Christmastide

The rain-shafts splintered on me
  As despondently I strode;
The twilight gloomed upon me
  And bleared the blank high-road
Each bush gave forth, when blown on
  By gusts in shower and shower,
A sigh, as it were sown on
  In handfuls by a sower.

A cheerful voice called, nigh me,
  'A merry Christmas, friend!' –
There rose a figure by me,
  Walking with townward trend,
A sodden tramp's, who, breaking
  Into thin song, bore straight
Ahead, direction taking
  Toward the Casual's gate.

THOMAS HARDY

Christmas Bells

I heard the bells on Christmas Day
Their old familiar carols play,
  And wild and sweet
  The words repeat
Of Peace on earth, Good-will to men!

And thought how, as the day had come,
The belfries of all Christendom
  Had rolled along
  The unbroken song
Of Peace on earth, Good-will to men!

Till ringing, singing on its way,
The world revolved from night to day,
  A voice, a chime,
  A chant sublime,
Of Peace on earth, Good-will to men!

Then from each black accursed mouth,
The cannon thundered in the South,
  And with the sound
  The carols drowned,
The Peace on earth, Good-will to men!

And in despair I bowed my head;
'There is no peace on earth,' I said,
  'For hate is strong
  And mocks the song
Of Peace on earth, Good-will to men!'

Then pealed the bells more loud and deep:
'God is not dead, nor doth he sleep!
  The Wrong shall fail,
  The Right prevail,
With Peace on earth, Good-will to men!'

HENRY WADSWORTH LONGFELLOW

Christmas Day. The Family Sitting

In the days of Caesar Augustus
   There went forth this decree:
Si quis rectus et Justus
   Liveth in Galilee,
Let him go up to Jerusalem
   And pay his scot to me.

There are passed one after the other
   Christmases fifty-three,
Since I sat here with my mother
   And heard the great decree:
How they went up to Jerusalem
   Out of Galilee.

They have passed one after the other;
   Father and mother died,
Brother and sister and brother
   Taken and sanctified.
I am left alone in the sitting,
   With none to sit beside.

On the fly-leaves of these old prayer-books
   The childish writings fade,
Which show that once they were their books
   In the days when prayer was made
For other kings and princesses,
   William and Adelaide.

The pillars are twisted with holly,
   And the font is wreathed with yew.
Christ forgive me for folly,
   Youth's lapses – not a few,
For the hardness of my middle life,
   For age's fretful view.

Cotton-wool letters on scarlet,
  All the ancient lore,
Tell how the chieftains starlit
  To Bethlehem came to adore;
To hail Him King in the manger,
  Wonderful, Counsellor.

The bells ring out in the steeple
  The gladness of erstwhile,
And the children of other people
  Are walking up the aisle;
They brush my elbow in passing,
  Some turn to give me a smile.

Is the almond blossom bitter?
  Is the grasshopper heavy to bear?
Christ make me happier, fitter
  To go to my own over there;
Jerusalem the Golden,
  What bliss beyond compare!

My Lord, where I have offended
  Do Thou forgive it me.
That so when, all being ended,
  I hear Thy last decree,
I may go up to Jerusalem
  Out of Galilee.

JOHN MEADE FALKNER

Christmas in Prison

From the Christian point of view there is no special problem about Christmas in a prison cell. For many people in this building it will probably be a more sincere and genuine occasion than in places where nothing but the name is kept. That misery, suffering, poverty, loneliness, helplessness and guilt mean something quite different in the eyes of God from what they mean in the judgement of man, that God will approach where men turn away, that Christ was born in a stable because there was no room for him in the inn – these are things that a prisoner can understand better than other people; for him they really are glad tidings . . .

DIETRICH BONHOEFFER
Letters and Papers from Prison

Christmas Nostalgia

There are people who will tell you that Christmas is not to them what it used to be: that each succeeding Christmas has found some cherished hope, or happy prospect, of the year before, dimmed or passed away, and that the present only serves to remind them of reduced circumstances and straitened incomes – of the feasts they once bestowed on hollow friends, and of the cold looks that meet them now, in adversity and misfortune. Never heed such dismal reminiscences. There are few men who have lived long enough in the world, who cannot call up such thoughts any day in the year. Then do not select the merriest of the three hundred and sixty-five, for your doleful recollections, but draw your chair nearer the blazing fire – fill the glass and send round the song – and if your room be smaller than it was a dozen years ago, or if your glass be filled with reeking punch, instead of sparkling wine, put a good face on the matter, and empty it off-hand, and fill another, and troll off the old ditty you used to sing, and thank God it's no worse . . . Reflect upon your present blessings – of which every man has many – not on your past misfortunes, of which all men have some. Fill your glass again, with a merry face and contented heart. Out upon it, but your Christmas shall be merry, and your New Year a happy one.

CHARLES DICKENS
Sketches by Boz

No Christmas

The Puritans came to power in 1640 but Christmas was not immediately abolished. The Presbyterians' dislike of the observance of Christmas finally erupted in 1644, when Christmas Day fell upon the newly appointed fast day, and an order was given on 19 December to suppress it.

Whereas some doubts have been raised, whether the next fast shall be celebrated, because it falls on the day which heretofore was usually called the feast of the nativity of our Saviour; the lords and commons in parliament assembled to order and ordain, that public notice be given, that the fast appointed to be kept the last Wednesday in every month ought to be observed, till it be otherwise ordered by both houses; and that this day in particular is to be kept with the more solemn humiliation, because it may call to remembrance our sins, and the sins of our forefathers, who have turned this feast, pretending to the memory of Christ, into an extreme forgetfulness of him, by giving liberty to carnal and sensual delights, being contrary to the life which Christ led here on earth, and to the spiritual life of Christ in our souls, for the sanctifying and saving whereof, Christ was pleased both to take a human life, and to lay it down again.

On Christmas Day itself Edmund Calamy preached before the House of Lords:

This day is commonly called Christmas-day, a day that has heretofore been much abused in superstition and profaneness. It is not easy to say, whether the superstition has been greater, or the profaneness . . . and truly, I think the superstition and profaneness of the day are so rooted in it, that there is no way to reform it, but by dealing with it as Hezekiah did with the brazen serpent. This year God, by his providence, has buried it in a fast, and I hope it will never rise again.

In Dessexshire as it Befel

In Dessexshire as it befel
A farmer there as I knew well
On a Christmas day as it happened so
Down in the meadows he went to plough.

As he was a ploughing on so fast
Our Saviour Christ came by at last;
He said, O man, why dost thou plough
So hard as it do blow and snow?

The man he answered the Lord with speed,
For to work we have great need,
If we wasn't to work all on that day
We should want some other way.

For his hands did tremble and pass to and fro,
He ran so fast that he could not plough;
And the ground did open and let him in
Before he could repent his sin.

His wife and children were out at play;
And all the world consumed at last.
And his beasts and cattle all died away
For breaking of the Lord's birthday.

ANONYMOUS

A Puritan Christmas

Dec. 25, 1696. We bury our little daughter. In the chamber, Joseph in course reads Ecclesiastes 3rd a time to be born and a time to die – Elisabeth, Rev. 22. Hanah, the 38th Psalm. I speak to each, as God helped, to our mutual comfort I hope. I ordered Sam to read the 102 Psalm. Elisha Cooke, Edw. Hutchinson, John Baily, and Josia Willard bear my little daughter to the Tomb.

Note. Twas wholly dry, and I went at noon to see in what order things were set; and there I was entertained with a view of, and converse with, the Coffins of my dear Father Hull, Mother Hull, Cousin Quinsey, and my Six Children: for the little posthumous was now took up and set in upon that that stands on John's: so are three, one upon another twice, on the bench at the end. My Mother lies on a lower bench, at the end, with head to her Husband's head: and I ordered little Sarah to be set on her Grandmother's feet. 'Twas an awfull yet pleasing Treat; Having said, The Lord knows who shall be brought hither next, I came away.

April 1, 1719. In the morning I dehorted Sam Hirst and Grindal Rawson from playing Idle Tricks because 'twas first of April; They were the greatest fools that did so. New England Men came hither to avoid anniversary days, the keeping of them, such as the 25th of Dec. How displeasing must it be to God, the giver of our Time, to keep anniversary days to play the fool with ourselves and others . . .

SAMUEL SEWALL

The holy feast of Widow Twankey

The traditions that have grown up around Christmas are rarely questioned — even though, on close inspection, they are very strange indeed. Take mistletoe, yule logs, and, perhaps the oddest of them all, pantomime.

Try explaining the concept of pantomime to a foreigner, and see how far you get before you are scratching your head at this extraordinarily popular phenomenon.

There is no doubt that panto is big business. Theatres up and down the land pull in all manner of soap stars, comedians, ex-celebrities, and the occasional bewildered American TV star from the '90s with a large tax bill to pay off. The link between the panto stories and Christmas is not clear.

The story of Christmas is left to primary schools to hack through. Toddlers in tea towels deal with the incarnation of Jesus, the Virgin birth, and the massacre of the innocents. The weighty stories of Mother Goose, Puss in Boots, and Babes in the Wood are for the adults to explore in greater detail.

The fact is that if you don't end up at a children's nativity play, the closest you'll come to the Christmas story during the season is the beginning of A Festival of Nine Lessons and Carols from King's (before the Baileys takes effect, round about Lesson Four).

In terms of storytelling at Christmas, pantomimes rule the roost. The stories have to be drawn from a small pool of traditional European folk-tales, which are then laced with references to The X Factor and 'He's behind you!' jokes.

But here's the really odd bit. The leading man, the prince or the hero, is traditionally played by a woman. And the leading woman, the dame, is played by a man. After all, what could be more Christmassy than cross-dressing?

These strange traditions have been at the front of my mind recently, because my daughter is two, going on three, and is already very excited about Christmas. And I don't know what to tell her.

The poor little girl is trying to piece together the traditions and customs in her head, but the odds are against her. She knows that Christmas is Jesus's birthday; and that all good things come from him. But she must be wondering why good things such as presents come from Father Christmas. She doesn't suspect the presents are from her parents, because why would they buy them, lie about them, and give the credit to a mysterious man who lives at the North Pole? The Santa story is much more plausible.

Except that we don't call him Santa in our house. It feels too American (even though it's Dutch). We don't call him St Nicholas or St Nick, either, lest we confuse St Nick with Old Nick — who are very different from each other, even though both wear a red suit.

So, we stick with the British version — Father Christmas, who lives in Lapland. He is the jolly, big, bearded man she's never met who creeps into her room in the middle of the night while she's sleeping.

This should, of course, be very alarming. We're not sure how this is going to go down with her — although if this Father Christmas leaves her some sweets and some stickers, she won't care whether she's been visited by St Nick, Old Nick, or Nicholas Lyndhurst.

I am not sure I can explain to her why we bring an entire tree into the house for a fortnight, but at other times of the year we restrict ourselves to flowers. Or why the tree is topped off with a fairy rather than an angel like the one in the Christmas story that we're meant to be celebrating.

And why do we pull crackers with truly dreadful jokes and hopelessly disposable toys inside? Why do we wear crowns made of yellow tissue-paper? Why do we put out nuts and dates in bowls, and then never touch them?

Best to say nothing. Likewise, I don't explain that we don't eat turkey at any other time of the year — the reason being that it isn't very nice, and that I'd rather eat the box that the stuffing came in.

On reflection, the whole traditional Christmas meal is bewildering. We drive across the country to be with our families and catch up with each other — and then eat a heavy, soporific meal: turkey, multiple root-vegetables, little sausagey things, bread sauce, redcurrant jelly, and stuffing. And alcohol.

A sorbet would be a sensible pudding. But no, it has to be Christmas pudding — a rich, fruit-based, heavy dark mass that we like so much we set fire to it. Then to the sofa. Perhaps it is nature's way of staving off arguments, because we're all too full and drowsy.

The other Christmas tradition, of course, is sitting down to watch Christmas *EastEnders*, which is usually a howling fight-fest. But this one is easy to explain. It's an act of charity on behalf of the BBC, reassuring the nation that, however dreadful your Christmas is, the one at Albert Square is even worse.

But the reality is that my daughter has no problem with any of these internal contradictions and oxymorons. She knows that Father Christmas isn't part of the Trinity, that Widow Twankey is a man, and that overeating on this scale is not acceptable all year round.

These things happen because they happen, and have always happened. Like the running of the bulls in Pamplona, or Trooping the Colour, or the Carling Cup.

My daughter, like all children at Christmas, is not going to worry about anything, because she'll be far too busy getting on with having a wonderful time. We could all learn from that.

JAMES CARY

Out upon Merry Christmas!

'A Merry Christmas, uncle! God save you!' cried a cheerful voice. It was the voice of Scrooge's nephew, who came upon him so quickly that this was the first intimation he had of his approach.

'Bah!' said Scrooge. 'Humbug!'

He had so heated himself with rapid walking in the fog and frost, this nephew of Scrooge's, that he was all in a glow; his face was ruddy and handsome; his eyes sparkled, and his breath smoked again.

'Christmas a humbug, uncle!' said Scrooge's nephew. 'You don't mean that. I am sure.'

'I do, said Scrooge. Merry Christmas! What right have you to be merry? What reason have you to be merry? You're poor enough.'

'Come, then returned the nephew, gayly. What right have you to be dismal? What reason have you to be morose? You're rich enough.'

Scrooge having no better answer ready on the spur of the moment, said, 'Bah!' again; and followed it up with 'Humbug.'

'Don't be cross, uncle.' said the nephew.

'What else can I be,' returned the uncle, 'when I live in such a world of fools as this? Merry Christmas! Out upon Merry Christmas! What's Christmas time to you but a time for paying bills without money; a time for finding yourself a year older, but not an hour richer; a time for balancing your books and having every item in 'em through a round dozen of months presented dead against you? If I could work my will,' said Scrooge, indignantly, 'every idiot who goes about with "Merry Christmas", on his lips, should be boiled with his own pudding, and buried with a stake of holly through his heart. He should!'

'Uncle!' Pleaded the nephew.

'Nephew!' returned the uncle, sternly, 'keep Christmas in your own way, and let me keep it in mine.'

'Keep it!' repeated Scrooge's nephew. 'But you don't keep it.'

'Let me leave it alone, then,' said Scrooge. 'Much good may it do you! Much good it has ever done you!'

'There are many things from which I have derived good, but which I have not profited, I dare say,' returned the nephew: 'Christmas among the rest. But I am sure I have always thought of Christmas time, when it has come round – apart from the veneration due to its sacred name and origin, if anything belonging to it can be apart from that – as a good time: a kind, forgiving, charitable, pleasant time: the only time I know of, in the long calendar of the year, when men and women seem by one consent to open up their shut-up hearts freely, and to think of people below them as if they really were fellow-passengers to the grave, and not another race of creatures bound on other journeys. And therefore, uncle, though it has never put a scrap of gold or silver in my pocket, I believe that it has done me good, and *will* do me good; and I say, God bless it!'

The clerk in the Tank involuntarily applauded: becoming immediately sensible of the impropriety, he poked the fire, and extinguished the last frail spark forever.

'Let me hear another sound from *you*,' said Scrooge, 'and you'll keep your Christmas by losing your situation.'

CHARLES DICKENS
A Christmas Carol

The Tranter's Christmas Party

The guests had all assembled, and the tranter's party had reached that degree of development which accords with ten o'clock p.m. in rural assemblies. At that hour the sound of a fiddle in process of tuning was heard from the inner pantry.

'That's Dick, said the tranter. 'That lad's crazy for a jig.'

'Dick! Now I cannot – really, I cannot have any dancing at all till Christmas-day is out,' said old William emphatically. 'When the clock ha' done striking twelve, dance as much as ye like.'

'Well, I must say there's reason in that, William,' said Mrs Penny. 'If you do have a party on Christmas-night, 'tis only fair and honourable to the sky-folk to have it a sit-still party. Jigging parties be all very well on the Devil's holidays; but a jigging party looks suspicious now. O yes; stop till the clock strikes, young folk – so say I.'

It happened that some warm mead accidentally got into Mr Spink's head about this time.

'Dancing,' he said, 'is a most strengthening, livening, and courting movement, 'specially with a little beverage added! And dancing is good. But why disturb what is ordained, Richard and Reuben, and the company zhinerally? Why, I ask, as far as that do go?'

'Then nothing till after twelve,' said William.

Though Reuben and his wife ruled on social points, religious questions were mostly disposed of by the old man, whose firmness on this head quite counterbalanced a certain weakness in his handling of domestic matters. The hopes of the younger members of the household were therefore relegated to a distance of one hour and three-quarters – a result that took visible shape in them by a remote and listless look about the eyes – the singing of songs being permitted in the interim.

At five minutes to twelve the soft tuning was again heard in the back quarters; and when at length the clock had whizzed forth the last stroke, Dick appeared ready primed, and the instruments were boldly handled; old William very readily taking the bass-viol from its accustomed nail, and touching the strings as irreligiously as could be desired.

* * *

'I like a party very well once in a while,' said Mrs Dewy, leaving off the adorned tones she had been bound to use throughout the evening and returning to the natural marriage voice; 'but, Lord, 'tis such a sight of heavy work next day! What with the dirty plates, and knives and forks, and dust and smother, and bits kicked off your furniture, and I don't know what all, why a body could a'most wish there were no such things as Chrismases...'

THOMAS HARDY
Under the Greenwood Tree

Christmas must go

Christmas is utterly unsuited to the modern world. It presupposes the possibility of families being united, or reunited, and even of the men and women who chose each other being on speaking terms. Thus thousands of young adventurous spirits, ready to face the facts of human life, and encounter the vast variety of men and women as they really are, ready to fly to the ends of the earth and tolerate every alien or accidental quality in cannibals or devil-worshippers, are cruelly forced to face an hour, nay sometimes even two hours, in the society of Uncle George; or some aunt from Cheltenham whom they do not particularly like. Such abominable tortures cannot be tolerated in a time like ours. That larger brotherhood, that truer sensibility, has already taught every spirited young lady (of sufficient wealth and leisure) to be thrilled at the prospect of having breakfast with a gun-man, lunch with a Sheik, and dinner with an Apache in Paris. It is intolerable that such sensibility should suffer the shock of the unexpected appearance of her own mother, or possibly her own child. It was never supposed that Parents were included in the great democratic abstraction called People. It was never supposed that brotherhood could extend to brothers.

Anyhow, Christmas is unsuited to modern life; its concentration in the household was conceived without allowing for the size and convenience of the modern hotel; its inheritance of ceremonial ignored the present convention of unconventionality; its appeal to childhood was in conflict with the more liberal conception; that Bright Young Things should always feel as if they were old and talk as if they were dull . . .

. . . Anyhow, it is unnecessary to extend the list or evidences that Christmas does not fit in with this fuller and more liberated life. Christmas must go. Christmas is utterly unsuited to the great future that is now opening before us. Christmas is not founded on the great communal conception which can only find its final expression in Communism. Christmas does not really help the higher and healthier and more vigorous expansion of Capitalism. Christmas cannot be expected to fit in with modern hopes of a great social future. Christmas is a contradiction of modern thought. Christmas is an obstacle to modern progress. Rooted in the past, and even the remote past, it cannot assist a world in which the ignorance of history is the only clear evidence of the knowledge of science. Born among miracles reported from two thousand years ago, it cannot expect to impress that sturdy common sense which can withstand the plainest and most palpable evidence for miracles happening at this moment. Dealing with matters purely psychic, it naturally has no interest for psychologists; having been the moral atmosphere of millions for more than sixteen centuries, it is of no interest to an age concerned with averages and statistics. It is concerned with the happiest of births and is the chief enemy of Eugenics; it carries along with it a tradition of voluntary virginity, yet it contains no really practical hints for compulsory sterilisation. At every point it is found to be in opposition to that great onward movement, by which we know that ethics will evolve into something that is more ethical and free from all ethical distinctions. Christmas is not modern; Christmas is not Marxian; Christmas is not made on the pattern of that great age of the Machine, which promises to the masses an epoch of even greater happiness and prosperity than that to which it has brought the masses at this moment. Christmas is medieval; having arisen in the earlier days of the Roman Empire. Christmas is a superstition. Christmas is a survival of the past.

But why go on piling up the praises of Christmas? All its gifts and glories are externally symbolised in that fact already sufficiently summarised; that it is a nuisance to all the people talking the particular nonsense of our own time. It is an irritation to all men who have lost their instincts; which is very truly the intellectual equivalent of losing their senses. It is a perpetual annoyance to the cads who are not only captains of industry, but captains of information and international news, and everything else in the present paradise of cads. It is a challenge to caddishness, because it reminds us of a more gracious world of courtesy; and of customs which assumed a sort of dignity in human relations. It is a puzzle to pedants whose cold hatred involves them in a continual contradiction; who are distracted between denouncing Christians because it is a Mass, or purely Popish mummery, and trying to prove at the same time that it is entirely heathen, and was once as admirable as everything else invented by the pirates of heathen Scandinavia. It stands up unbroken and baffling; for us one thing, for them a confusion of inconsistencies; and it judges the modern world. Christmas must go. It is going. In fact it is going strong.

G K CHESTERTON
G K's Weekly, 7 Dec 1933

☆

To Candlemas and Beyond

Why art thou troubled, Herod?

Why art thou troubled, Herod? what vain fear
  Thy blood-revolving breast to rage doth move?
Heaven's King, who doffs himself weak flesh to wear,
  Comes not to rule in wrath, but serve in love;
Nor would he this thy feared crown from thee tear,
But give thee a better with himself above.
    Poor jealousy! why should he wish to prey
    Upon thy crown, who gives his own away?

Make to thy reason, man, and mock thy doubts;
  Look how below thy fears their causes are;
Thou art a soldier, Herod; send thy scouts,
  See how he's furnished for so feared a war.
What armour does he wear? a few thin clouts.
  His trumpets? tender cries. His men, to dare
    So much? rude shepherds. What his steeds? alas,
    Poor beasts! a slow ox and a simple ass.

RICHARD CRASHAW

God face to face

It is telling that most people seem to think that happiness lies in what we have, whether that be a Porsche or a loving family. Not a great deal of opinion has been voiced yet about whether it might, instead, be linked to who we are, and what we have become, and how we are resourced internally as human beings.

MARK OAKLEY

The New-Yeeres Gift

Let others look for pearle and gold,
Tissues, or tabbies manifold:
One onely lock of that sweet hay
Whereon the blessed babie lay,
Or one poore swadling-clout, shall be
The richest new-yeeres gift to me.

ROBERT HERRICK

New Year's Eve

Of all sound of all bells – (bells, the music nighest bordering upon heaven) – most solemn and touching is the peal which rings out the Old Year. I never hear it without a gathering-up of my mind to a concentration of all the images that have been diffused over the past twelvemonth; all I have done or suffered, performed or neglected, in that regretted time. I begin to know its worth, as when a person dies. It takes a personal colour; nor was it a poetical flight in a contemporary, when he exclaimed –
'I saw the skirts of the departing Year.'
It is no more than what in sober sadness every one of us seems to be conscious of, in that awful leave-taking. I am sure I felt it, and all felt it with me, last night; though some of my companions affected rather to manifest an exhilaration at the birth of the coming year, than any very tender regrets for the decease of its predecessor. But I am none of those who –
'Welcome the coming, speed the parting guest.'
I am naturally, beforehand, shy of novelties; new books, new faces, new years, – from some mental twist which makes it difficult in me to face the prospective. I have almost ceased to hope; and am sanguine only in the prospects of other (former) years. I plunge into foregone visions and conclusions. I encounter pell-mell with past disappointments. I am armour-proof against old discouragements. I forgive, or overcome in fancy, old adversaries. I play over again *for love*, as the gamesters phrase it, games for which I once paid so dear . . .
The elders, with whom I was brought up, were of a character not likely to let slip the sacred observance of any old institution; and the ringing out of the Old Year was kept by them with circumstances of peculiar ceremony. – In those days the sound of those midnight chimes, though it seemed to raise hilarity in all around me, never failed to bring a train of pensive imagery into my fancy ...

CHARLES LAMB

A New-year's gift sent to Sir Simeon Steward

No news of Navies burnt at seas;
No noise of late spawned *Tittyries*,
No closet plot, or open vent,
That frights men with a Parliament:
No new device, or late found trick,
To read by the Stars, the Kingdom's sick:
No gin to catch the State, or wring
The free-born Nostrils of the King,
We send you; but here a jolly
Verse crowned with Ivy and with Holly:
That tells of Winter's Tales and Mirth,
That Milk-maids make about the heart,
Of Christmas sports, the Wassail-bowl,
That's tossed up, after *Fox-i' th'hole:*
Of *Blind-man-buff*, and of the care
That young men have to shoe the *Mare*:
Of Twelfth-tide Cakes, of Peas and Beans,
Wherewith ye make those merry Scenes,
When-as ye choose your King and Queen,
And cry out, *Hey for our town green.*
Of Ash-heaps, in the which ye use
Husbands and Wives by streaks to choose:
Of crackling Laurel, which fore-sounds
A Plenteous harvest to your grounds:
Of these, and such like things, for shift,
We send in stead of New-year's gift.
Read then, and when your faces shine
With bucksome meat and capering Wine:
Remember us in Cups full crowned,
And let our City-health go round,
Quite through the young maids and the men,
To the ninth number, if not ten;

Until the fired Chestnuts leap
For joy, to see the fruits ye reap,
From the plump Chalice, and the Cup,
That tempts till it be tossed up:
Then as ye sit about your embers,
Call not to mind those fled Decembers;
But think on these, that are to appear,
As Daughters to the instant year:
Sit crowned with Rose-buds, and carouse,
Till *Liber Pater* twirls the house
About your ears; and lay upon
The year (your cares) that's fled and gone.
And let the russet Swains the Plough
And Harrow hang up resting now;
And to the Bagpipe all address;
Till sleep takes place of weariness.
And thus, throughout, with Christmas plays
Frolic the full twelve Holy-days.

ROBERT HERRICK

Ring out, wild bells

Ring out, wild bells, to the wild sky,
　The flying cloud, the frosty light:
　The year is dying in the night;
Ring out, wild bells, and let him die.

Ring out the old, ring in the new,
　Ring, happy bells, across the snow:
　The year is going, let him go;
Ring out the false, ring in the true.

Ring out the grief that saps the mind,
　For those that here we see no more;
　Ring out the feud of rich and poor,
Ring in redress to all mankind.

Ring out a slowly dying cause,
　And ancient forms of party strife;
　Ring in the nobler modes of life,
With sweeter manners, purer laws.

Ring out the want, the care, the sin,
　The faithless coldness of the times;
　Ring out, ring out thy mournful rhymes
But ring the fuller minstrel in.

Ring out false pride in place and blood,
　The civic slander and the spite;
　Ring in the love of truth and right,
Ring in the common love of good.

Ring out old shapes of foul disease;
　Ring out the narrowing lust of gold;
　Ring out the thousand wars of old,
Ring in the thousand years of peace.

Ring in the valiant man and free,
  The larger heart, the kindlier hand;
  Ring out the darkness of the land,
Ring in the Christ that is to be.

ALFRED LORD TENNYSON

New Year's Eve

'I have finished another year,'said God,
　　In grey, green, white, and brown;
I have strewn the leaf upon the sod,
Sealed up the worm within the clod,
　　And let the last sun down.'

'And what's the good of it?' I said,
　　'What reasons made you call
From formless void this earth we tread,
When nine-and-ninety can be read
　　Why nought should be at all?

'Yea, Sire; why shaped you us, "who in
　　This tabernacle groan" –
If ever a joy be found herein,
Such joy no man had wished to win
　　If he had never known!'

Then he: 'My labours – logicless –
　　You may explain; not I:
Sense-sealed I have wrought, without a guess
That I evolved a Consciousness
　　To ask for reasons why.

'Strange that ephemeral creatures who
　　By my own ordering are,
Should see the shortness of my view,
Use ethic tests I never knew,
　　Or made provision for!'

He sank to raptness as of yore,
　　And opening New Year's Day
Wove it by rote as theretofore,
And went on working evermore
　　In his unweeting way.

TOM HARDY

What the bird said early in the year

I heard in Addison's Walk a bird sing clear
'This year the summer will come true. This year. This year.

'Winds will not strip the blossom from the apple trees
This year, nor want of rain destroy the peas.

'This year time's nature will no more defeat you,
Nor all the promised moments in their passing cheat you.

'This time they will not lead you round and back
To Autumn, one year older, by the well-worn track.

'This year, this year, as all these flowers foretell,
We shall escape the circle and undo the spell.

'Often deceived, yet open once again your heart,
Quick, quick, quick, quick! – the gates are drawn apart.'

C S LEWIS

Keeping Resolutions

Every man naturally persuades himself that he can keep his resolutions, nor is he convinced of his imbecility but by the length of time and frequency of experiment. This opinion of our own constancy is so prevalent, that we always despise him who suffers his general and settled purpose to be overpowered by an occasional desire. They, therefore, whom frequent failures have made desperate, cease to form resolutions; and they who are become cunning, do not tell them. Those who do not make them are very few, but of their effect little is perceived; for scarcely any man persists in a course of life planned by choice, but as he is restrained from deviation by some external power. He who may live as he will, seldom lives long in the observation of his own rules.

SAMUEL JOHNSON

Lord, when the wise men came from far

Lord, when the wise men came from far,
Led to the cradle by a star,
Then did the shepherds too rejoice,
Instructed by thy angels' voice;
Blest were the wise men in their skill,
And shepherds in their harmless will.

Wise men in tracing nature's laws
Ascend unto the highest cause;
Shepherds with humble fearfulness
Walk safely, though their light be less;
Though wise men better know the way,
It seems no honest heart can stray.

There is no merit in the wise
But love (the shepherds' sacrifice).
Wise men, all ways of knowledge past,
To th' shepherds' wonder come at last;
To know, can only wonder breed,
And not to know, is wonder's seed.

A wise man at the altar bows
And offers up his studied vows
And is received; may not the tears
Which spring too from a shepherd's fears,
And sighs upon his frailty spent,
Though not distinct, be eloquent?

'Tis true, the object sanctifies
All passions which within us rise;
But since no creature comprehends
The cause of causes, end of ends,
He who himself vouchsafes to know
Best pleases his creator so.

When then our sorrows we apply
To our own wants and poverty,
When we look up in all distress
And our own misery confess,
Sending both thanks and prayers above,
Then though we do not know, we love.

SIDNEY GODOLPHIN

Story

For us there are no certainties, no star
blazing our journey, no decisive dream
to reassure hurt hearts or warn us when
it's time to move. The shepherds, harassed men,
are given answers to the questions they
have never thought to ask, told where to go
and what to look for. We try out our way
unlit with angels, wondering 'How far?'
Yet in the story we find who we are:
the baby is told nothing, left to grow
slowly to vision through the coloured scheme
of touch, taste, sound; by needing learns to pray,
and makes the way of the flesh, dark stratagem
by which God is and offers all we now.

JENNIFER DINES
For The Time Being

Ceremonies for Candlemas Eve

Down with the Rosemary and Bays,
   Down with the Mistletoe;
Instead of Holly, now up-raise
   The greener Box (for show).

The Holly hitherto did sway;
   Let Box now domineer;
Until the dancing Easter-day,
   Or Easter's Eve appear.

The youthful Box which now hath grace,
   Your houses to renew;
Grown old, surrender must his place,
   Unto the crisped Yew.

When Yew is out, then Birch comes in,
   And many Flowers beside;
Both of a fresh, and fragrant kin
   To honour Whitsuntide.

Green Rushes then, and sweetest Bents,
   With cooler Oaken boughs;
Come in for comely ornaments,
   To re-adorn the house.

Thus times do shift; each thing his turn does hold;
New things succeed, as former things grow old.

ROBERT HERRICK

The Ceremonies for Candlemas Day

Kindle the Christmas Brand, and then
   Till Sun-set, let it burn;
Which quenched, then lay it up again,
   Till Christmas next return.
Part must be kept wherewith to tend
   The Christmas Log next year;
And where 'tis safely kept, the Fiend,
   Can do no mischief there.

ROBERT HERRICK

The Child Jesus

Hail, blessed Virgin, full of heavenly grace
Blest above all that sprang from human race
Whose heaven-saluted womb brought forth in one
A blessed Saviour, and a blessed son;
O! what a ravishment 't had been to see
Thy little Saviour perking on thy knee!
To see him nuzzle in thy virgin breast!
His milk-white body all unclad, undrest;
To see thy busy fingers clothe and wrap
His spradling limbs in thy indulgent lap!
To see his desperate eyes, with childish grace
Smiling upon his smiling mother's face!
And, when his forward strength began to bloom,
To see him diddle up and down the room!
O, who would think so sweet a babe as this
Should e'er be slain by a false-hearted kiss!

FRANCIS QUARLES

Mary remembers

Once, measuring his height, he stood
  Beneath a cypress tree,
And, leaning back against the wood,
  Stretched wide his arms for me;
Whereat a brooding mother-dove
Fled fluttering from her nest above.

At evening he loved to walk
Among the shadowy hills, and talk
  Of Bethlehem;
But if perchance there passed us by
The paschal lambs, he'd look at them
In silence, long and tenderly;
And when again he'd try to speak,
I've seen the tears upon his cheek.

JOHN BANISTER TABB

Has Nothing Changed?

The angel of the Lord appeared to Joseph in a dream and said, 'Get up, take the child and his mother and escape to Egypt'. (Matthew: 2.13)

They travelled through the night
Into Egypt, the stars were clear,
As they are now,
The moon was incredibly near,
The mountains rocky,
The way dusty,
As they are now,
There are those who,
For one reason or another,
Travel into Egypt, today.

As the sun came up, cocks crowing,
It would have become hot,
The donkey's head would
Droop lower,
Ears forward, and the mother
Would have drawn
Some shade over the baby's head,
As they do now.

Into the desert shimmer
The village they reached
Would have dozed
At midday, the old men squatting
In the shade, and a woman carrying
A water jar on her head
Would have greeted them,
As she greeted me today.

It's a long walk to the well,
And there is no piped water
To this village;
Slowly I seek the shadow of a wall.
Did the small donkey foal
Out on the glittering sand,
Lick its mother's urine
For moisture then, As it does now?
Has nothing changed, nothing at all?

MARGUERITE WOOD

All in the Morning

It was on Christmas Day,
And all in the morning,
Our Saviour was born,
And our heavenly King:
And was not this a joyful thing?
And sweet Jesus they called him by name.

It was on New Year's Day,
And all in the morning,
They circumcised our Saviour
And our heavenly King:

It was on the Twelfth Day,
And all in the morning,
The Wise Men were led
To our heavenly King:

It was on Twentieth Day,
And all in the morning,
The Wise Men returned
From our heavenly King:

It was on Candlemas Day,
And all in the morning,
They visited the Temple
With our heavenly King:

It was on Holy Wednesday,
And all in the morning,
That Judas betrayed
Our dear heavenly King:
And was not this a woeful thing?
And sweet Jesus we'll call him by name.

It was on Sheer Thursday,
And all in the morning,
They plaited a crown of thorns
For our heavenly King:

It was on Good Friday,
And all in the morning,
They crucified our Saviour,
And our heavenly King:

It was on Easter Day
And all in the morning,
Our saviour arose,
Our own heavenly King;
The sun and the moon
The did both rise with him,
And sweet Jesus we'll call him by name.

ANONYMOUS

Index of Sources and Acknowledgements

The publisher has attempted to contact all copyright holders. We would be happy to rectify any omissions in future editions should the copyright holder come forward.